Speaking for Effect

The Strategy of Successful Speaking

Library of Congress Cataloging-in-Publication Data:

Number: 89-92282

Author: Young, Michael

Title: Speaking for Effect

First edition

ISBN 0-9624503-0-8

Printed in the United States of America.

Published by:

Speaking for Effect

P.O. Box 966

Montrose, California

Acknowledgments

Thanks to the following for their contributions:

Cheryl for - Everything.

Bill Bradly for - That first "big" opportunity and continuing support.

Darrel "Dodie" Garner for - Proofreading.

Gary Hofer for - Polish and editing.

Gina Hoiseth for - The first critical look and review.

Phyllis Ortman for - Editing and excellent suggestions.

Toastmasters International and MWD WaterMasters club #445 for - The arena to develop and practice.

AST Research and Hewlett-Packard for - First class tools.

And

The "Speaking for Effect" team for - Proving it all works!

Cheryl, Eddie, Kelly, Marti, Michael, Mike, Tom, Victor.

Table of Contents

Preface

Two friends who hadn't seen each other in many years, met at a class reunion. As they discussed their current lives and old memories, the conversation soon turned to the teachers they remembered who had most influenced them and contributed to their development. The History, English and Gym classes were first remembered. Both then recalled the lectures by various teachers on the value of hard work, persistence and continued education. Funny how both friends had become leaders in their fields.

They were soon joined by a third class mate who was also very successful. The same question was posed to the newcomer. A few moments of thought produced the name of their speech teacher, who had taught all of them the skills of effective communication. They recalled the requirement to lead a class discussion and the several oral presentations each gave. They shared their memories and their stories. Then a moment of reflection as they silently remembered how those skills had led to their individual successes. Yes, their expertise in their chosen fields had given them exposure, but there were many that had similar educations and experiences. The hard work and long hours had contributed, yet there was still something else. It was strange that their fields of endeavor varied so widely, yet all three credited the same teacher and the same class. Maybe it was the teacher's commitment, enthusiasm, the material or maybe the skills.

Eyes scanned the room, perhaps the teacher was close by and long overdue thanks could be given. Another thought crossed the minds of the three individuals. Maybe there were still more lessons to be learned.

INTRODUCTION

At the begining of our careers, technical skills are the most important. Later communication skills become the dominant factor. In fact, we believe that the ability to communicate effectively is the most powerful skill a human can possess. Successfully acquiring, providing and exchanging information is a key to achievement in business and to the enhancement of social and personal relationships.

Communication takes place in a variety of arenas: written, verbal, non-verbal, electronic and print. However, the verbal arena is most used and has the most potential to effect our lives and careers. For that reason we will concentrate on verbal communication in the following pages. The skills involved are easily learned, yet largely overlooked within our educational system. People can complete their formal education with but a single speech class. Even the most highly educated can't possibly achieve a high level of proficient speaking without study and work.

History reflects that the world is dramatically changed by great communicators.

Patrick Henry asked for "liberty or death"; Susan B. Anthony secured women's suffrage; John F. Kennedy promised men on the moon; Martin Luther King, Jr., had a dream; Lee Iacocca revived Chrysler and the Statue of Liberty. Now in the age of television and instant global information transfer, we have unlimited opportunities to influence others around the world.

Oral communication is gaining popularity due to instant global communication. Unfortunately the written word is losing much of its audience. Teleconferencing, video cassettes and an array of dazzling computerized graphics support the speaker's message.

A few years ago, Time magazine named the computer its "Man of the Year." Yes, computers are entering every phase of human life; and people who can access and apply "micro-chip power" are in great demand. However, we sincerely believe that people who can speak effectively one to one, one to small groups or one to thousands, hold the key to success.

We have a heritage of open exchange of ideas and information, the right to question, and the right to call to action. Through these elements of free speech, we have the ability to affect change.

These skills are available and can be learned. But it is not easy. It takes work. Yet many have done it through awareness, commitment and persistence. Public speaking, formerly referred to as the ancient art of rhetoric, must be carefully studied and deliberately mastered.

This book will provide the tools and techniques that will move you toward mastery. It is a compilation of extensive research, experiences in training speakers, and years of actually speaking. Actual successful and unsuccessful experiences provide the examples. Of course, names have been changed to protect the guilty and the innocent. The keys are here in these pages. Read them. Think about them. Use them. Step through the door.

Chapter 1

ABOUT SPEAKING

"The journey of a thousand miles must begin with the first step."

- Lao Tzu

Speaking is a learned skill

Learned skills are mastered first by awareness of need, next by acquisition of knowledge, and finally by practice.

Most people know they need speaking skills, and some may purchase books hoping to find the answers; yet few take the time to practice. On the other hand, if you as an individual do not possess the technical knowledge, you can practice for years without significant improvement. You may know how to accomplish a skill and you may practice that skill, but without perception of a need to improve, progress and accomplishment will again be slow. All three components, perception of need, technical knowledge and consistent practice, must be present to master any skill-based performance.

In these pages you will find the knowledge to master the skill of speaking. You will also receive as much explanation of the need to become proficient as can be packed into a book. You must only supply the practice.

The need for proficiency can be found in three basic areas: the requirement to give a talk; the desire to effectively get ideas across; and the desire for personal improvement in an area that is necessary for success. In fact, the quality of our life is in direct relation to the quality of our communication. This is true in both personal and professional life. Unfortunately, many people fail to recognize a basic need to improve communication skills. Your reading of this book hopefully reflects an awareness of that need. Once someone recognizes the need, one can begin to acquire the knowledge.

The knowledge in this book is structured around the individual parts of speaking. Like building a house, you start at the foundation and work your way up. Each step in design and construction must be in the correct order. We have studied the individual components of speaking and the order in which they are performed. We call it the "Strategy of Speaking." The strategy contains all the components and the sequence in which they must be acomplished. Like a combination lock, not only are all the numbers needed, but they must be in the right order for the lock to open.

The strategy was obtained by studying expert speakers both in business and government. These experts all prepared and delivered presentations in the same way. We also studied speakers who were good, but not quite expert. They used many of the same components, but not all and not always in the same sequence. This research led to an idea, "What if we copied the method of the experts?"

We taught a group of 20 good speakers the components and the correct sequence of the strategy used by the expert speakers. We then had them prepare and deliver a presentation using the experts' strategy. It worked. All the good speakers improved, and sometimes it was dramatic. These, as you remember, were all good speakers. Next we tried poor speakers. Again it worked. This time the improvement was spectacular. We found that the performance skills involved in speaking not only required knowledge of the techniques and practice at applying that knowledge, but we also discovered that the best speakers use mental concentration and focusing techniques, which many people overlook.

These mental skills and the speaking strategy are the new and different things offered in this course. We believe that never before have these elements been brought together. They form the newest developments in speaking performance improvement.

In order to gain the most from these new tools, we urge you to be here and get involved. Please don't jump ahead or you may lose the correct order of the strategy. We also urge you to try the techniques of mental preparation. These are the extras that most speaking courses and books don't teach. Speaking is a performance skill that requires close coordination between mind and body much like sports which also requires high levels of mental concentration. In all mind-body skills, the top performers use mental preparation techniques. Give them a fair try, and you will be amazed at how well they work.

The Beginning

It all starts when we first know we are going to speak. At that time, we must start an orderly progression toward our objective, and our mental attitude must support us along the way. These things are easy to say but where do we start to insure our success? Our modeling of the experts showed that you must start preparing earlier than most people believe. Simply writing down the information about the purpose of the talk will begin the process. When and where, of course, are the first bits of information, along with how many people and how long the speech should be. Put these notes and any other information on the subject in a separate speaking file. This is one of the small things that can help you get started in the right direction. Knowing the purpose of the talk and about the audience is the information needed before any writing begins. These key bits of information allow you to quickly assemble material that supports the purpose and will be meaningful to your audience. These techniques are covered extensively in the next two chapters.

Organizing the presentation in a way that supports the purpose and is meaningful to the audience is part of a mind set that states, "This is for them, not just what I want to say." This is an important difference. Poor speakers tend to just focus on themselves. The better speakers have an outward focus. This mind set carries through the entire speaking process. The ineffective group of speakers are thinking only of themselves and how they look and sound. The effective group concentrates on the audience and the message. This focus begins on the organizational process and continues through the actual delivery.

Basics

How we turn an idea into an understandable concept and then communicate that idea to others is the foundation. We must have command of a concept before we can shape the message. We have constructed a model that represents the process of communicating effectively. Let us study this model and see how we can use the information to improve our skills. By understanding the entire communication process, we can then begin to apply specific techniques to improve our effectiveness in community, personal and business situations.

The Circle of Understanding

The model begins with an idea, concept or perhaps an important piece of information. You have the great idea partially

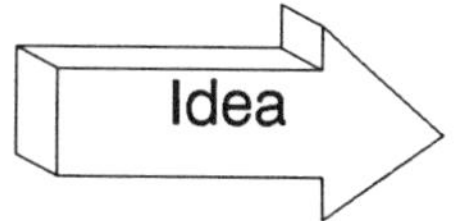

or fully formed in your mind. You may perceive the idea in its entirety and it is crystal clear. Perhaps the idea is a quickly developing internal dialogue, or it could be just a strong feeling. The task is to break the concept into its component parts and formulate a word description of those components. This description must be such that it will allow the receiver to re-assemble all the components into the complete idea as originally conceived, without error.

To communicate an idea, we need to turn it into words and transmit it to others. It is estimated that as much as 30% of a concept can be lost turning an idea into words.

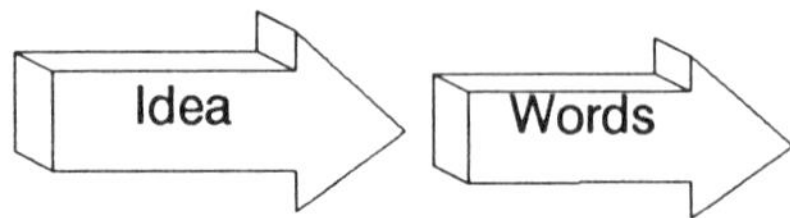

Almost all of us have had the problem of not being able to find just the right words to describe our ideas. There are over 600,000 words in the English language. The average adult uses about 5,000 words in their speaking vocabulary. Some words are quite common to certain people's vocabulary. The word definitions are exacting. However, they fail to realize not all listeners have the same definition or understanding of meaning. Each of us has our own 5,000 words. The situation is further complicated because even common words mean different things to different people. Take a word like "fast" - what does the word "fast" mean to you? If you said "to move quickly," you were right; or if you said "not to eat," you were also right. "Moving with a wild crowd" or "gluing material together" and a few other definitions are also right. Differences in word interpretation can cause misunderstanding.

It is said that the ear is a gateway to the mind. Whether that is true or not, we know that when speaking, much of the information is received through the ear.

The words form the cornerstone of our message. They are the substance and contain most of the information we are trying to communicate. It is important that people not only hear all the words, but also the vocal inflections, in order for them to receive the complete message.

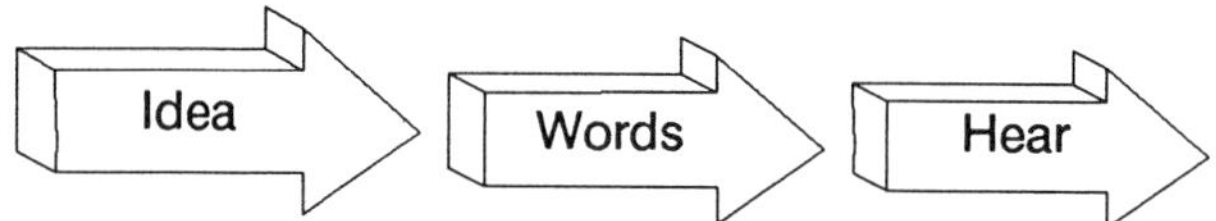

Unfortunately distractions interfere with the message being received in its entirety. This interference causes much of our information to become lost. People have things on their minds, which can cause lack of attention. Many times noises or people passing by temporarily disrupt attention. These disruptions always seem to occur just at the moment that a vital piece of information is being transmitted. Another factor is that we can think at about 600 words-per-minute, yet we speak at only about 150 words-per-minute. This allows a kind of time sharing. People can drop out and think about many things while someone is speaking thus missing information that may be critical to the presentation.

Sometimes we are not even speaking the same language dialect as the people with whom we are trying to communicate. Even though we seem to have a common language, we all come from different backgrounds and that contributes to our different interpretation of words. Along with these factors, there are many other things which can interfere with the listening process, such as passing around material, the temperature of the room or a multitude of other distractions. All these plus personal problems or illness can interfere with individual receptivity.

To be an effective communicator, we need to know how our message was received and how it was interpreted. To obtain this information, we need feedback. This is the connection between perception and reality. We need to ask people what they think we said or meant. This sometimes takes a bit of doing; however, it is worth it. As a speaker our problem is difficult. We can't ask everyone in an audience what they think we said. We must use other methods of receiving feedback. One prime method involves awareness of the audience's reaction to our message. The smile or the frown, the open or closed body position, the yawn or the lack of attention are all non-verbal clues that can give us the information we need.

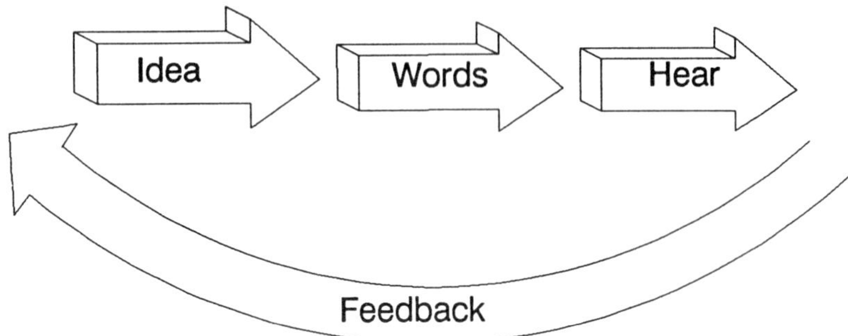

In informal speaking situations, we should ask people what they heard and understood, and wait for their reply. We shouldn't accept non-expressive responses. We must get them to explain their perceptions of what we said. We can occasionally paraphrase or prompt to encourage them to express themselves. If they misinterpreted the message, we can rephrase, clarify or simplify.

A few years ago a labor problem seemed to be developing within a large airline's staff in Denver. After years of good labor relations, things had taken a turn for the worse. Absenteeism was up, turnover was up and the number of grievances filed was up.

Upon visiting the operation, the problem was soon evident. While touring the facilities with a first-line supervisor, we came across a baggage cart in one of the subsurface corridors. It was out of place and the supervisor called over a nearby worker. "What *&#@ is this doing here? Who left this #@&% cart here?" The worker's reply was, "I don't know." After the denial, instructions were given as to where the cart was to be taken. It seemed as if minutes of detailed directions were given.

To us, the visitors, it was very confusing. Then the supervisor, in an obviously irritated manner, asked if the worker understood and if there were any questions. However, the body language of the supervisor (arms folded and threatening) said, "You better not question me." The worker's reply was barely audible -- a semi-nod of the head and a grunt. The worker was then dismissed to return the cart to the appropriate place.

Asking the supervisor if he thought the worker understood the instructions, we got the message loud and clear that any questioning of supervisors was not expected. Still following up, the supervisor was left behind and the worker was tracked down. When asked whether or not he understood the instructions, he indicated that he not only didn't understand, but that he was going to hide-out and skip the afternoon's work because he didn't want to get caught again.

This illustrates a problem many of us have. When under pressure and in a hurry, we tend to shut off the feedback necessary to know whether our message got through. We must make an extra effort to keep the channels open for questions and suggestions. Once we know how our message is perceived, we can take the last step, the one that makes all the difference.

Follow-up completes the circle

When we know how our message is coming across, we can reshape it, if necessary, to insure the desired interpretation. We simply re-transmit the message in a different way. We sometimes need to repeat instructions in a slow and specific manner. Asking the listener to take notes or repeat the message verbally will help. At times we may need to use illustrations or stories to reinforce the message. This re-transmitting or second chance increases the opportunity for improved listener understanding.

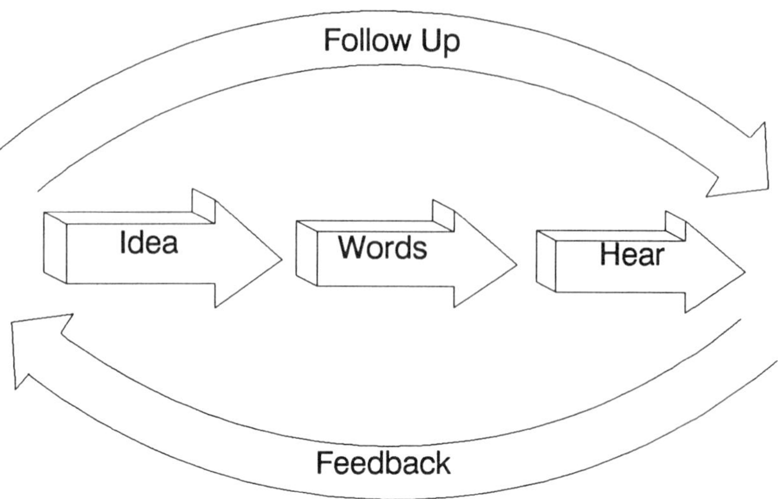

Follow-up is neglected far too often when we are in a hurry or under pressure. Yet, with correct follow-up, our effectiveness increases and we begin to improve rapidly. Remember that the quality of our lives is in direct relation to the quality of our communication.

Summary

Speaking is a learned performance skill that in order to master requires an awareness of need, an acquisition of knowledge, and dedicated practice. The knowledge includes a study of how the experts prepare, how they think and how they deliver the message. This also involves the mental "psyching-up" skills. Finally, the basic understanding of the communication process begins with realizing that what we may perceive clearly, others may have trouble understanding. The reasons are different interpretations of words and interference in the communication channels. The circle of understanding is the foundation on which we shall build our skills.

Chapter 2

OVERCOMING NERVOUSNESS

To conquer fear is the beginning of wisdom."

-- Burtrand Russell

In this chapter we will deal with the anticipation and apprehension many people feel when they have to deliver a speech. We'll show the correct way to channel your energy to insure it is focused in the right direction. This knowledge will help control any fear or nervousness.

Most people, at one time or another, are uncomfortable getting up and speaking before a group of people. It's common to be afraid of public speaking. In 1973 a survey was done to determine people's fears for *The Book of Lists.* Fear of heights, fear of snakes and the fear of dying were listed. The most frequently mentioned fear, was that of speaking before a group. It was even greater than the fear of dying or cancer. Maybe that's because most of us don't have to deal with those fears right now. Yet, if we want to keep our job or perhaps get a promotion, we may have to give a presentation. Some may then say "they would rather die."

Nervousness is one of the outlets for the energy our bodies produce. Unfortunately, this uncontrolled use of energy can be detrimental to communicating our message.

Many people will say that nervousness is normal and to be expected while speaking. Yes, there is indeed a certain build up of energy before a speech. We need that extra energy to speak effectively, but nervousness is a misdirection of that energy.

Our bodies constantly produce energy. When we are about to attempt any performance, our bodies begin to produce the required energy. Because our bodies can't store it, production of the necessary energy should closely follow the body's needs. When seated, waiting to speak, our energy requirements are quite low. Then as we rise to make a presentation, the energy requirements shoot up. During a presentation increased energy is required. How much depends on the speakers style and subject matter.

Athletes, actors and other high-performing individuals experience a similar energy build-up before an important event. If left unchecked and undirected, it can be detrimental to the desired outcome.

Unfortunately, many times the mind causes the body to prepare too early, which results in excess energy available while waiting, and too little energy available later when speaking.

The amount of energy is controlled mainly by the hormone adrenaline. This prepares us for whatever may occur. In ancient history our ancestors needed this to deal with life-and-death situations. They had to either fight or run to survive. This fight-or-flight need was met by increased adrenaline in their blood streams. This provided great strength or great speed, depending on the need.

The natural increase of energy before a presentation sometimes shows up as jitters, sweaty palms and a host of other physical manifestations. This is simply the body's way of burning off excess energy. Incorrectly, we sometimes interpret these feelings as fear, which further increases the energy production beyond what is needed and depletes reserves for later use. We misinterpret these reactions because they are the same kinds of feelings we have experienced when faced with very threatening situations. Of course, speaking is certainly not a life-threatening situation.

Whether a speaker, a high-power business executive or an athlete, this extra energy must be controlled or directed during the performance or event. When we rise to speak, the energy our bodies have been creating energizes our presentation. Without this energizing, our listeners might fall asleep or become bored and disinterested. Danish philosopher Soren Kierkegaard said, "*To venture causes anxiety but not to venture is to lose oneself.*"

The following graph shows how energy is produced before and during a speech. This plot shows a profile of the energy needed and the actual energy our bodies produce. The difference between the two plots indicates the excess and the shortage of energy that can be experienced both before and during speaking.

Energy vs. Time for Speakers

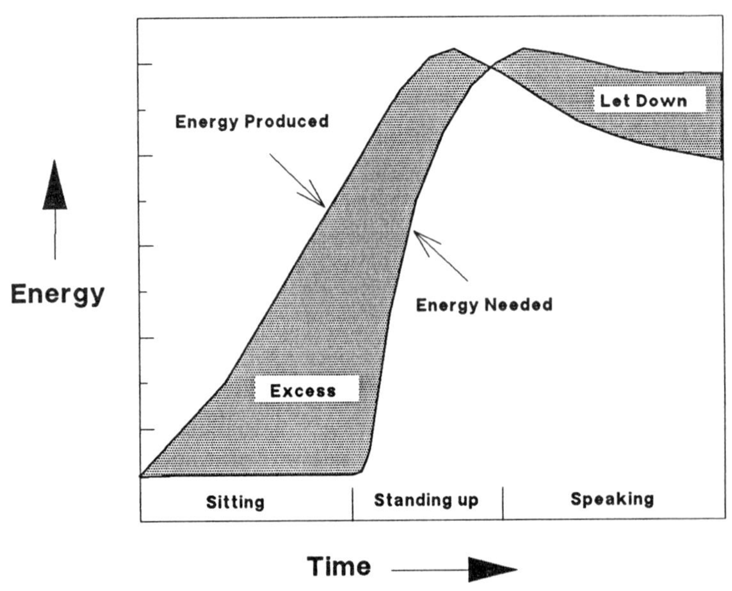

While speaking, the requirement for energy remains fairly high. If the body has used up its adrenaline supply too soon, there will be a letdown. It may result in a feeling that we're losing it or just not doing a good job. This letdown feeling can undermine confidence just as effectively as the jitters can, before speaking. We don't want to eliminate the build up of energy, just have it more closely follow our bodies' needs. How do we control the normal pre-speaking excess energy build up and save our reserves for our presentation? First we can intellectually try to understand the factors that cause nervousness. This helps prevent misinterpretation of what is happening and allows us to control some of the elements which can cause unnecessary anxiety. Next, we can control our breathing. And finally, we can prepare ourselves mentally. These last two engage the mind just before speaking. They control the body's energy production and are covered in Chapters 8 and 9.

Let's begin with intellectually understanding what kinds of things we might fear about speaking. Actually there are only three basic things to fear: 1. The Material. "Maybe they'll think I don't know what I'm talking about. There are those that know more about the subject than I do." 2. The Audience. We're afraid of the people listening to the speech. "What will they think of me? What if they don't like me?" 3. The Performance. Your inner-voice tells you that you're going to stand up and make a fool of yourself.

If we could conquer those three, we'll have nothing to fear!

The Material

Why do we fear the material? Usually you're not asked to speak unless you are an expert on the subject or at least very knowledgeable. Most of us will be giving presentations on what we do; our specialty, our work, our community or our ideas. What if we don't have all the information? What if we don't have all the facts? What do we do? Research!

A book or a report can, in a few hours, teach what may have taken someone a lifetime to discover. Books and reports can have all the facts and figures needed. And, of course, information is a key to power. In this information age, we have, at our fingertips, all the needed resources. All we need to do is take the time to read and research.

What if there is someone in the audience who still knows more about the subject than you? Call on that person before the presentation, "Larry, I know you're an expert on computers, how about giving me some help?" or just before the presentation you can go to Larry and say, "I'm giving a report. I know you have a great deal of insight on this, can I call on you to help out if I get stuck?" Larry will feel good because he has been recognized as the expert. He most likely will give the information needed, and you'll have an expert to quote. That's how to turn a potential critic into a friend and supporter.

We have the opportunity to acquire the knowledge. But it still takes more. We have to prepare and not at 9:30 the night before the presentation. Many people try this and fall asleep by 9:32.

Prepare in private and you will be rewarded in public. Vince Lombardy once said, "*It's not the will to win that counts, it's the will to prepare to win that makes champions.*" When you have to speak, decide you are going to do a good job and make a commitment to yourself, "I have the knowledge of my subject or I can get it. All I need to do is take the time to prepare the material." However, as you begin organizing the material, fear number two may get in your way.

The Audience

"What if they don't like my material or anecdotes? What if they don't like me?" Realize that you must establish rapport with your audience. People accept ideas much more readily from people they like and trust. Research the group. Find their likes and dislikes. Then you can organize and design your speech around their interests and you will begin to create rapport with your audience.

We sometimes can be intimidated by an audience, but usually not by friends. Arrive early, make a friend or two, get to know their interests. Then during the speech say, "As Tom and

I were talking earlier about _______(your subject)." Show interest in them, and the audience will show interest in you. Recognizing a member of the group lets them know that you care about their interests as well as the subject. Also, try to dress like the audience. Match their style. For additional tips on dress see the Appendix.

Commitment to sharing the message also helps overcome fear of the audience. Believing in what we are saying is the cornerstone of commitment. If you cannot be committed to the message, then do not give the presentation. This is your integrity check.

You really don't need to fear the audience if you establish rapport with them and commit yourself to the message. They are pulling for you to succeed. Don't be embarrassed if you drop your pencil, stumble over a word or lose your place. All of us make mistakes. If you do err, you create empathy and the audience will actually support you. If you act embarrassed after a miscue, so will your audience. But if you shrug it off and continue, your listeners will be impressed. Sometimes, mix-ups occur that only you have knowledge of; you left your special map back at the office or you forgot part of your speech. Don't let your listeners in on your small problems. Stay cool. They will never know.

The Performance

Many people have a little voice inside that says, "You're going to make a fool of yourself," or "You'll lose your place and people will laugh at you." Yet , think about it, how many people would laugh when someone loses their place or forgets a line? Not many. Most of us would have empathy for the speaker.

But, as a speaker don't think you can "wing it" and avoid practice. If you don't practice, you should be afraid. Some people have to practice more than others. Do what's right for you. The important thing is to practice at least a few times, and do it standing up and out loud. In business, people avoid practice by using the excuse that they are too busy. Make time!

What if you were in a bowling match against a professional and you had not practiced. Would you fear your performance and feel nervous? Of course, most people would. If you practiced everyday for 6 months would you feel more confident about your performance? Certainly. It's the same with speaking. Practice in front of a mirror, with a tape recorder, to your dog. Phyllis Diller became a success by rehearsing everyday at the laundromat.

A few years ago, in the World's Championship of Public Speaking sponsored by Toastmasters International, there were nine contestants. Each was a champion from their part of the world. One of the contestants was in his 70's. The title of his speech, "Retirement Never." As he stood on the platform ready to speak to over 2,000 people, there was tremendous pressure. He believed so strongly in his message and sharing it with the audience that he didn't notice the lavaliere microphone slipping from around his neck and falling to the stage floor. The audience did notice that his voice level dropped. A member of the audience picked up the microphone and handed it to him. He smiled, nodded and confidently finished his speech to a rare standing ovation. His commitment to the message, rapport and preparation allowed him to win the world championship.

Let's analyze what happened. He acted as if nothing serious had occurred. It was no big deal. The audience felt empathy. They wanted him to succeed. They understood how he felt and were pulling for him. Think about your feelings when a speaker has a problem, aren't you hoping everything will work out O.K.?

Summary

Whether you are giving a presentation to a board of directors, at a management meeting or to a group of scouts, you need to understand and control your nervousness or energy build-up by mastering the three fears of speaking.

Material - Master the material by finding the information through research and then preparing it for the audience.

Audience - Touch and hold thc audience by creating rapport and being committed to the message.

Performance - Excellence comes from Practice, Practice, and more Practice.

Overcome these three fears, and you'll have nothing to fear. You'll be the master of your performance and have the key to delivering a dynamic presentation.

Chapter 3

ESTABLISH YOUR PURPOSE

"The secret of success is consistency of purpose." -- *Benjamin Disraeli*

While the circumstances, subjects and audiences may change, the one variable that remains constant is the long, thoughtful and sometimes painstaking process of clearly understanding and defining your purpose or objective before the actual speech construction. What is the desired response to the presentation?

In this chapter you will be given a plan, a map, a guide, for your journey to discover your destination. This journey may be very successful for you, your company, or your group; or, it may fail disastrously. A captain rarely sets sail without a destination. "The result of your communication is the response it receives regardless of your intentions." Think about it. The responsibility for getting the desired response lies with the assumption that you know the response you wish to achieve. If you do not know your purpose, how will you know if you have succeeded?

Theory

Ideal communication accomplishes the purpose the communicator intended. Realistically, ideal communication occurs when the presenter's message is understood and acted upon in the way the sender desires. With a vague objective or an unclear purpose, the ideal response is lost. The effort of communicating may have to be repeated many times, and sometimes the desired objective is never achieved. The purpose of any communication is the target. Without a clearly definded target the communicator doesn't know which direction to head.

Questions

To clearly define our purpose we must ask certain questions. The first is simple, but even good speakers sometimes find it the most complex: "Why am I giving this speech, what is my exact objective?" Again, you must have a well defined answer before proceeding. Be sure to ask this question of anyone giving you a speaking assignment. Do not accept an off-the-cuff remark such as, "Well whatever you want," or "Just tell them about the project." The fullest and most succinct answer to the simple question, "What is my purpose?" will point the speaker directly to format, material required, organization, length, style and possible visual aids needed. Some examples of basic purposes are: sell a product or project, change attitudes or opinions, provide information, obtain participation, and commitment. These are just a few of the possible purposes.

More Questions

The following questions are as simple (or as complex) as the first. They will be your guide in designing your presentation. You may remember them as the five W's: WHO, WHAT, WHERE, WHEN, WHY. And there's a sixth W - "WHOA!!!" Whoa or stop must follow each of the other questions to insure the process is carried out carefully and completely. The question, WHY requires identification of the communication's purpose and must be answered first. The question "WHO is this presentation for?" (Audience Analysis), will be discussed in detail in the following chapter. WHAT is the general subject and will be more clearly defined when the purpose is known. WHERE and WHEN should be clearly understood and should be part of the original information gathered.

Examples

Sadly we don't have to think too hard to find examples of speakers who either forgot or never knew their purpose.

Quinn, the newly elected president of a local service club, was asked to address a group of community officials. He began with, "I'm not sure why they asked me to speak, but let me tell you about the challenges I see in the year ahead." His speech wandered and rambled so badly it seemed as if the year would end before the speech. Quinn obviously didn't understand the need of a definite purpose.

Bill, a friend who is an attorney, delivered a very detailed and serious presentation to a group of potential investors about the cause-and-effect of draining a swamp in northern Florida. Unfortunately, by the end of his speech, he had forgotten his purpose and found himself knee deep in alligators. You get the message. If you don't keep your purpose in mind, you too, may find yourself knee deep (or higher) in alligators.

Summary

Define your purpose! "Why am I giving this talk? What is my objective?" Answer these questions carefully and you will know your destination. This will allow you to quickly assemble the information and facts necessary to support your purpose. Much like sailing a ship, without a clear or definite course, you will find neither port nor support. Whatever your subject, knowing the purpose and the desired response is the first step in the process of effective communication.

Chapter 4

AUDIENCE ANALYSIS

"You need to put the right bait on the hook" -- *Mark Twain*

In the preceding chapter on Purpose, we discussed the importance of asking a few simple questions. These questions, when given thoughtful and complete answers, help the speaker prepare a dynamic presentation. Some people are amazed that speech preparation and proper presentation require the presenter to think first of the listeners. After all, isn't the main concern what we say? No, the main concern is what the audience wants to hear and how we can get them to listen. The more we know about our audience, in advance of our presentation, the better are our chances of successful communication.

A few years ago in Tulsa, Oklahoma, a Quality Circle group had to make a presentation to upper management. They had developed a new method of computer memory management that could save their company between $100,000 and $200,000 annually. It did involve an initial investment and a change in procedures. The idea was excellent and well thought out.

They decided to make the presentation a team effort, even though some of the circle members were very apprehensive about speaking before groups. When the big day arrived, they were all ushered into a large presentation room. At the back of the room where the management team sat, the lights were dimmed. The spot lights were focused on the platform where the circle group stood. As one can imagine, even the most experienced speakers were wilting under the pressure. Needless to say things didn't go well and the suggestion was turned down. In that situation, there was no prior knowledge of the audience's understanding or interest in the subject. Consequently, the presentation, although prepared and rehearsed, did not make a connection with the audience. Without this connection, the material was only partially relevant to the group. Those who did not have a connection with the presentation tended to "drop out".

A few months later, we had an opportunity to work with the group just before they were to receive a second chance. They knew their idea was sound and were still committed. Their purpose was clear, yet they still didn't know their audience. We worked out a strategy to obtain information about the management team. Two circle members were assigned to research company biographic information. They also interviewed people who had worked with members of the management group. Lastly, the circle group hosted an informal get together for everyone before the presentation. Coffee and rolls were served. Informal conversations were used to establish rapport and to connect with current interests of the management group.

The information gathered allowed the presentation to be tailored to the interests and knowledge of the audience. Examples were relevant to past and current experiences and interests of the management team. The circle group also capitalized on the strength of its individual members. Presentation duties were re-evaluated, with stronger speakers taking a lead roll. Members who were more comfortable working behind the scenes, were assigned those duties where they provided exceptional support. The presentation was a big success and the project saved the company a great deal of money. Yes, the group put extra effort into the second presentation, but the extra effort proved most effective. They could have debated back and forth among themselves about what to say the "next time." Yet, by trying to understand their audience, they were able to prepare the material so that the audience understood the message. Then they delivered it in a way that the audience wanted to hear. That's working smarter, not just harder.

Who won? Everybody! The company saved money. The circle members earned a reputation as effective communicators who were able to relate to management. They could see the big picture rather than just the limits of their specialty. After seeing and hearing the circle group's commitment and their demonstration of team work, the company expanded the quality circle concept.

Opening a window of receptivity with an audience comes as a direct result of how effectively we understand them and prepare our message in their terms. Little communication can take place until the presenter captures and holds the would-be listener's attention. The immediate task is to convince our listeners that the time they spend listening is time well spent. If we as presenters, address the following questions when preparing our presentation, the chances for success will dramatically improve.

1) What do they want at this point in time?
2) What are their concerns?
3) What do they know?
4) What do they understand?
5) What do they not understand?

Presentations that arouse interest will gain the listener's attention. A good presentation does not command thought on a certain subject, but rather stimulates the listener to think about the subject. A good presentation calls for action. However, the presentation must also convince the listeners that action is required. This is done by giving the subject and proposed action some real thought. Then prepare stories and examples to which the audience can relate. By customizing the material into terms that are meaningful to the listeners, we can capture their interest. The audience analysis chart at the end of this chapter provides a quick reference guide. Depending on the nature of the presentation, we may want more information in some areas and less in others. However, all presentations deserve some conscious advance audience analysis, even if it is the same group of fellow workers or club members to whom we have been giving weekly or monthly updates for years.

Summary

Good presentations give listeners ideas to build upon and help them sort out problems or challenges and find solutions. In order to build an effective message, we must relate to the listener. It is not just saying what we think people want to hear. It is saying something in a way that people will want to listen. Information gathered in the audience analysis increases immeasurably our chances of preparing the message in a way that people will listen, even if it's not what they want to hear. This also improves our chances of getting the desired results. Good audience analysis provides us with valuable insights and allows us to prepare an effective presentation.

AUDIENCE ANALYSIS CHART

Information Needed	Why It's Needed
Reason for Talk (see chapter on Purpose)	How formal What they expect What they need Relate to the occasion
Format	Place on the program During or after AM/PM meal. Liquor served. Time allocation Questions and answers Appropriate dress
Number of People	Room size Type of visual aids and size Electrical outlets Equipment needs Number of hand outs
Occupation	Level of expertise Organizational rank Experience Interests Decision makers or technical Relevant examples
Attitudes: Professional/Personal	Regional Establish rapport Type of approach Prior speakers on subject Discover strong feelings Find common bond Avoid unnecessary controversy or conflict
Education Level	Word choice (jargon) Idea density Their expertise
Age	Find their values Be relevant Level of complexity Appropriate examples

Chapter 5

CONTENT

"Words are the fingers that mold the mind, the person who can master them is the magician."

-- Daniel Webster

The content of the presentation is the heart of the message. To assemble the content is to first determine the purpose (Chapter 3), and then understand the needs of the audience (Chapter 4). The last component is the information and support material that is used to deliver the message. This chapter will provide the packaging, but you will have to provide the substance of the message. The following categories will help in formulating the content. They all have been proven effective in getting the listener's attention and winning acceptance of ideas.

Personal Experience

Personal experience fosters credibility. When a speaker has personally experienced something, it is more easily accepted as proof. If this experience can be connected with a situation the listeners may be facing, a linkage is created. Credibility can be enhanced by using the experiences of some other group or company. However, this is limited to how closely the company is related to the general business area of the listeners and how closely the core idea can be connected to the experience. An example would be another company of similar size which purchased a computer system. What type of system was chosen? Why was the particular model chosen? What was their experience with that selection?

Evidence

Not all presentations need strong evidence, but the great majority can benefit from additional support. People often say their work speaks for itself; they don't need to use this technique. Still, think about the basics of transferring information. Some people will absorb information immediately, while others require more information, perhaps presented in a different way. This is the extra evidence we are referring to.

Each person has their own way of evaluating information, rejecting what they don't believe and accepting other bits and pieces. The same information or evidence may not convince everyone. But, while people are very different and their methods of evaluating information are different, by using a few of these techniques, you can improve your chances of reaching the majority of listeners. Presenting information without considering these techniques is like always using a hammer even though a screw- driver sometimes may be more appropriate.

Experts

Credibility can be established by the use of outside experts who have already established personal credibility and who support the idea or premise you are presenting. Their credentials, accomplishments or statements are used to support your idea. Using a Tom Peters' quote from his book, "*In Search of Excellence,*" which supports your point or a Peter Drucker study, which examined a situation similar to one you're facing, are effective in reinforcing your idea or point of view.

Facts

Facts, of course, are very important, widely used and in many instances, over used. A few well-chosen pieces of information are more useful than a bushel basket of trivia. Direct examples from a related situation or similar situation can add support. Statistics are an important part of support. Although statistics and numbers can be manipulated and misleading, they also can form the hard evidence to support your case. The number of facts used is dependent on the audience. Engineering, financial, or technical people will require more details than a typical management group. This is where the analysis of the audience, before preparing the presentation, will provide the necessary information to correctly design the mix of material.

Stories

Stories convey messages in ways dry facts never can. They engage us emotionally, physically, and intellectually. As children we heard fairy tales which taught us many of life's lessons. This continues, as we grow older, with elaborate anecdotes which are effective in communicating ideas. Most of us can remember stories in which we almost lived the experience. Maybe we were scared and squirmed in our seats, or the sadness of the story actually brought tears to our eyes. Stories hold the audience's attention, while at the same time reinforcing the message.

The best stories are true life experiences. Things that have happened to us or to others. Stories can be modified to suit the actual presentation. However, this artistic license should not be taken too far unless we inform the audience that we tailored the story to better illustrate our point.

Metaphors can be effectively woven into stories so that the story contains messages that can have lasting effects far beyond their apparent significances. Metaphors can be terms, analogies, or full stories. Usually the message is not readily apparent, yet people make connections between the metaphor and some current situation. Consequently, metaphors deliver a concealed message that will have a powerful effect upon the listener.

Anecdotes give us the additional advantage of sending the message to the audience a second time in a different way, thus doubling the opportunity of getting the message across. It won't seem redundant. It will be refreshing, entertaining and will make the difficult seem easier to understand.

Visual Aids

Visuals (covered in Chapter 11) are one of the most important parts of a speech. They provide direct and indirect benefits to the speaker and the listener. The most obvious advantage is that visuals can show how things actually are: a photograph, model or drawing. Visual aids also help get the speaker to start preparing before the last minute. This is particularly helpful for those who tend to procrastinate. They also keep the speaker on track rather than wandering off on tangents. The listener, in turn, benefits from the engagement of the sense of sight. We are a visually oriented society, which accounts for the fact that listeners obtain about 55% of a speaker's message through visual input. If we try to carry our message without visuals, we risk losing the attention of the people in the audience. Visual aids also help the listeners who drop out to quickly re-enter the speaker's train of thought. Unfortunately, most people are easily distracted, either by disturbances or by the mind's preoccupation with other thoughts. When a new visual is displayed, the audience can quickly reengage with the speaker.

Summary

Before assembling the material, know your purpose and understand the needs of the audience. This allows you to gather, organize, and deliver the message in a way that accomplishes the desired result. Depending on the audience, use a mix of facts, expert support, stories and supportive material.

The experienced speaker uses visual aids to reinforce, restate and entertain. Visuals can dramatically improve the speaker's chance of getting the message across. A study by the Wharton School of Business indicated that visual aids significantly improve understanding and retention of information. Those who don't use visuals are limiting the tools available to them. It's like comparing a flight of stairs with an elevator. Both will allow us to get to the top floor. However, one takes a long time and requires much effort, while the other is quicker and more efficient. Which one would you choose to deliver the goods?

Chapter 6

HOW TO ORGANIZE

"A good plan today is better than a perfect plan tomorrow." *--Anonymous*

There are as many ways to organize a speech as there are ways to build a house. When designing a house a good architect will first determine the purpose of the house and then learn about who will occupy it. That forms the basic design parameter. Then blue prints, or a set of plans, will be developed. Then, and only then, will construction begin.

A well-designed speech will consider the purpose and the audience. Next the blue print should be developed. The blue print is the organizational structure that will be developed. It evolves from a broad perspective to a very refined structure.

The outlining process should begin with several large sheets of paper. Use a single sheet for each of the three parts of the speech: the opening or introduction, the body and the close.

The OPENING or introduction should clearly state the subject and purpose of the speech. The BODY should reflect main ideas or concepts. The CLOSING should reflect what you want your listeners to know, think, feel or do as a result of your presentation. Using large sheets of paper will allow you to rearrange your ideas or concepts many times. This will insure that the logic and sequence are correct. After concluding the large outline process, reduce the outline to a single page. There is a one-page outline format at the end of the appendix. Try it a few times and determine if it is right for you.

Remember, the opening attracts attention and previews the information that will be presented. We should tell the audience what we're going to tell them. This lets the audience know where they're going. Next, tell them the message in the body of the presentation. This will be the bulk of the information. Lastly, pull it together with a closing. Summarize what you just told them. This all seems simple enough. However, there are a number of ways to organize within that general format, depending on what we wish to accomplish. These special formats will be covered later in this chapter. An example of the general format and a description of the terms follow:

Standard Design

Introduction: Gets attention and focuses on the subject.

GET ATTENTION

a. Startling or interesting fact or statistic.

b. Provocative quotation, story, joke or anecdote.

c. Whatever is used, make it relate.

TELL STATEMENT: Preview the speech.

a. List the main points.

b. State what action you want them to take.

c. Paraphrase the central ideas.

d. The more specific you are, the better your audience can follow.

Body: The heart of the speech. This is where we tell them what we want to tell them.

a. Points needed to make the idea clear.

b. Main points supported by examples and illustrations.

c. Organized using the logic of the point.

d. Only three major points if possible.

Transitions: Signposts that lead the audience.

a. Establish relationships among the various parts of the speech.

b. Use connecting words or phrases.

c. Use internal summaries which bridge gaps between main points.

d. Physical movement or changing visual aids can signal a transition.

Conclusion: Summarizes the main points and leaves your audience feeling good about you and your speech. Reminds them what you told them.

a. If the introduction used a quotation you may want to close with a related quotation or repeat the original.

b. Tell the audience what you want them to think, feel or do (call for action).

Each presentation should have a specific point of view. That is defined by the answers to the purpose and audience questions. By keeping to those guidelines as we write and design our presentation, we will build a strong, coherent and congruent message, a message that will achieve our objective. Below are a sample of ways we can organize depending on what we want to accomplish and what seems to relate to the subject.

Other Designs

- Chronological: past, present, future.
- Sequential: first, second, third.
- Key Word spell out: P.I.G. pride, integrity, guts.
- Slogan: stop, look, and listen.
- Persuasive: interest, need, desire, action.
- Get Attention: why bring that up, example, so what.
- Ethos, Pathos, and Logos: credibility, emotions, reason.

Each of these stock designs works in the appropriate situation. Note that most of them use three main points. More can be confusing. If you have to use more than three main points, be careful to keep the audience with you. This can be accomplished by using clear transitions that summarize the point just made and indicate the relationship to the other points or ideas already presented.

The following organizational structures are designed for specific business situations. They are effective at accomplishing their intended outcome. Of course they aren't the only way to handle a situation, so they can be modified, changed, or adjusted to incorporate material as needed. Be creative and use your own corporate culture to determine what will be effective in each case.

Specific Types

Report on a project status:

- State project's goal and outline program
- Describe important achievements to date
- List major items of work remaining
- Describe approaches to unsolved problems
- Express confidence that goals will be met

Recommend a course of action:

- Explain need
- What will happen if nothing is done
- Outline proposed plan
- List benefits of action
- Describe how to implement an action

Propose an approach to a problem:

- State problem
- Outline alternatives and their drawbacks
- Describe proposed approach and its benefits
- Describe objections and how to answer them
- Describe how to implement the approach

Sell a product:

- Review customer's requirements
- Describe product and how it meets needs
- Tell why it is better than the competitor's
- List other important features
- Explain availability and call for action

<u>Sell a service:</u>

- Review customer's requirements
- Explain advantages of your service
- Describe service, cost and availability
- Tell why you are uniquely qualified to provide the service
- Tell how to obtain service

Summary

Each house has a foundation, a framework and a roof. Within that broad description lies a great variety of individual floor plans. So it is with our speeches. Depending on what we wish to accomplish, each will have a different format. We suggest that you use only three main points in any speech you make.

A well-organized speech avoids haphazard or illogical idea development so that listeners can follow easily and build on the ideas presented. This will insure everyone reaches the conclusion and/or have the reaction desired.

Chapter 7

PRACTICE

"A theorist without practice is a tree without fruit." --*James Ross*

The key to success in any skill is practice. To become good at a sport or game, practice is required. Try to remember your first attempt at bowling, golf, tennis, swimming, or bicycle riding; slipping, missing, struggling your way through the experience. Then if you kept at it, you improved, at first slowly then even more rapidly. Speaking before a group is a learned skill, similar to these examples.

Remember watching a child learn to walk? He falls the first few times, but with practice he finally masters a series of steps. There are a certain number of tries required before achieving a high level of competence. It's the same in speaking. The learning curve requires a certain number of speaking experiences before a speaker can feel comfortable and confident delivering a presentation.

Many people have had a bad speaking experience, so they avoid it and don't complete the required number of practice experiences. This prolongs the time required to master the skill. In fact, it may never be mastered if too few practices occur or too much time elapses between experiences. As stated earlier, there are a certain number of times a skill must be practiced to achieve mastery. This number will vary with each individual and skill level. Since most of us probably don't want to become a world class orator, the number of speaking experiences needed to reach a credible skill level will be reasonable. However, if we take too long between speaking experiences, we can forget what we've learned. Or if we don't receive useful feedback, the time required for mastery will be substantially extended. The following factors will help preparing for the big day.

How

Practice should include the complete speech using any visual aids. It should be done at least twice, more if many changes are made in the presentation. The use of a tape recorder allows us to hear how our presentation sounds. It also gives a way to review the speech before the actual presentation. Rehearsing the opening and closing once or twice extra will help the first few minutes go smoothly and insure that the closing will deliver the impact desired.

Time

Set aside time for practice. This usually means a few days and sometimes a few weeks before the big event. Many people spend so much time writing out the presentation, there is little time left for practice. There are people who begin their rehearsal late the night before or ten minutes before they go on. Push the paper and pencil aside and practice. Your time will be better spent practicing than any other way.

Environment

The best place to practice the speech is where it will be given. Certainly not every rehearsal has to take place at the exact location. That may not even be possible, but one or two rehearsals there will give you an edge. This includes practicing with the equipment and visual aids. This is vital because a piece of balky equipment can not only break the continuity but also reduce your confidence. Flip charts that won't flip or slides that don't slide are the mark of an unprepared speaker. Don't let it happen to you!

An example is Mary, who did an excellent job of preparing flip charts with great visual symbols and colors. Unfortunately, she didn't take time to practice with the easel that held her beautiful charts. Her opening was good with a preview of the talk. Then came her pride and joy - the charts. As she reached for the cover sheet, she noticed they were a little high for her 4-foot 10-inch frame. A slight hop was required to uncover the first masterpiece. This soon became a jump, then a leap. This would have been a great performance for a National Basketball Association slam dunk contest, but not so good for a business presentation. What a shame for such a talented person to lose effectiveness because of the few minutes it would have taken to practice with the easel. The next time, Mary went to the room and tested the equipment. Then she insisted on a saw and now all the easels are a little shorter. Practice and determination can do wonders.

Physiology

Duplicating body position and voice level will increase the effectiveness of practice. Standing up, as we would while giving a talk, and speaking gives us experience with gestures and verbalization. We can't duplicate the speaking posture by sitting down or repeating our talk silently. Those conditions are so far removed from the actual speaking experience, that practice in this fashion is nearly useless. Standing also allows us to breathe as we would in the actual presentation. Our physiology must match the experience as closely as possible. Children can't learn to walk sitting down nor can they learn to speak by internal verbalization.

Summary

Of all the factors contributing to our development as a speaker, actual practice is the most often neglected. Mental rehearsal is important and is discussed in the chapter on Psyching-Up. Still, it can't totally make up for lack of actual practice. Don't cheat yourself, your company or your group. Set aside time for rehearsal. Use a cassette recorder, turning the cassette over after each run through. This will allow you to listen to the talk in your car on the way to the big event. Not driving? Use a walkman. Don't have one? Get one.

Remember, the key to skill development is practice, practice and more ___________________!

Chapter 8

PSYCHING - UP

"Open your inner eye, there is a world within." *-- William Shakespeare*

Speaking has three general components. The first, of course, is the message. The second is delivery skills. The third is the mental process that controls our ability to construct and then deliver an effective message. This chapter will concentrate on those mental processes.

The quality of our performance is governed by the amount of energy we apply and how it's focused. To speak successfully we need to have the correct amount of energy available and focus it precisely. Focusing mental energy requires quieting the inner voice and directing our attention to the situation at hand.

In sports there are thousands of examples showing how athletes prepare themselves mentally for competition. These mental techniques, generally referred to as psyching-up, are: self-talk, visualization, and performance triggers.

Strangely, few people in business or the scientific fields use these concepts and techniques. In those areas, many people believe that only education, experience and hard work produce results. However, our research and actual experience have proven the effectiveness of these mental techniques for improving performance.

In business, other people question using sports techniques and methods. Some people are skeptical or have not used the methods before, but read on with an open mind and try these skill-enhancement techniques. Many people already use some of these techniques and are simply unaware of the process. This chapter identifies, describes and gives strategies on how to implement them. Use them and your speaking will improve dramatically.

Performance

Past performances help construct our self-image, which, in turn, controls our self-talk. It forms a circle, each part reinforcing the other. If a performance was poor, our self-image is lowered. Our self-talk then reflects our current self-image, which in turn, controls our next performance. This can be an upward or downward spiral depending on our latest information and current self-image. There are two methods of modifying this continuum. The first is controlling the inner voice.

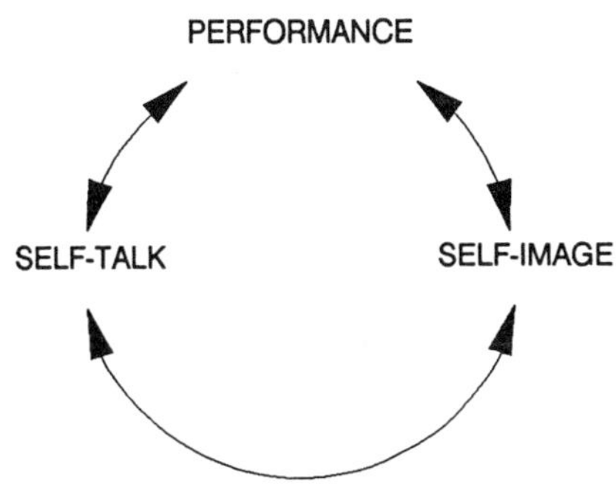

Controlling Inner Voice

All of us have self-talk or what we call an inner-voice. It can be our best friend or our worst enemy. This voice knows all about us, whether we're afraid or confident, nervous or calm. It can also be very vocal. Self-talk has two components, past performance and self-image.

Consciously changing the inner voice message can change the self-image and thus modify performance. "I'm unprepared and will forget my material," is replaced by "This will be great. This is just the information they need." Your energies now will focus on enthusiasm and excitement instead of on nervousness. It's not only all right, but important to say something positive, even if it's partly false. Control your inner voice by saying supportive comments as you prepare. Then just before you speak, build confidence with inner voice reinforcement for that extra edge.

In a sport, such as basketball, the inner voice is vital when a player approaches the free-throw line. His inner voice can either tell him, "I missed the last one. I hope this will be better," or "Right into the basket, smooth as silk."

The first statement ties up the player, with anxiety and nervousness. The second command supports the desired outcome. The high jumper can say, "That's too high, I'll never make it", or "One, two, three, jump, lift and over the top." Which statement will make a winner? It's the same with speaking. Self-talk controls expectations and performance. But what if we still have doubts?

Visualization

Sometimes we have had such bad experiences that it's hard to keep our self-talk positive, or we need something to break that downward spiral. That breakthrough strategy comes with visualization, "The Master Skill." It can change a losing image into success.

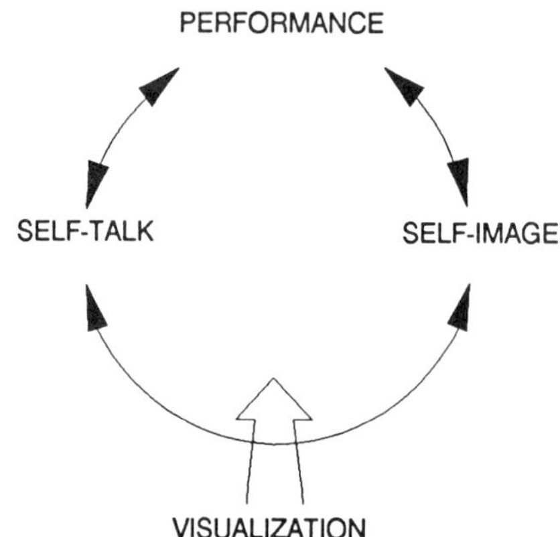

Creating vivid mental representations of desired outcomes is one of the most effective techniques available. Although referred to as visualization, it involves all the senses. Along with supportive self-talk, visualization separates the well-conditioned and practiced player from the champions. It's also what separates the good speakers from the great ones.

Pause for a moment. Think of the scent of fresh cut grass. Close your eyes and picture a country scene at sunrise. Hear the distant sound of a train whistle. Feel the light touch of a morning breeze blowing through your hair. Next try picturing yourself in a speaking situation just before you are to speak. See the room, feel the temperature of the air and feel the chair against your body. Hear your name called. See yourself rise with confidence. Now you face the audience and deliver the speech of your life. It was great. You can feel it inside. Hear the words of praise. Smile with the inner satisfaction of a job well done.

This exercise involves use of all the senses. For some this is easy. Others may find it very hard, but, as with many of the resources available to us, the effort to master it will be well rewarded. Stop right now and try it.

Again sports give us measurable examples of the power of visualization. Jack Nicklaus, famous golfer and winner of most major tournaments at least once, said that before every shot he forms a picture of the expected flight of the ball, the trajectory and landing. Even in practice he follows this rule. Conrad Hilton always said that he pictured owning hotels long before he actually did. Thomas Watson, founder of I.B.M., was once asked when he knew his company would be so big. "Right from the start I could see it," was his classic reply. Bruce Jenner, Olympic decathlon champion, pictured every movement of every event before he won the gold medal. He saw himself on the victory stand and heard the roar of the crowd. He felt the weight of the medal around his neck. He planned and practiced every move, both physically and mentally. He was so committed and convinced that he would win the gold, that he had someone waiting for him at the finish line with the little American flags he would carry around the track after his final victory.

Visualization equals success in both sports and business. Yet, sometimes in business people rely only on facts and numbers. However, the most successful realize that the more tools they have available, the more they enhance their potential. Those who use the tool of visualization, seem to have that extra edge.

Performance Triggers

We live in a stimulus/response world. Many things we do are unconscious, as in the urge we feel when the smell of fresh popcorn or cookies permeates the air. These responses are caused by performance triggers or anchors. These triggers or anchors are sensory stimuli linked to a specific event or physical state. They can be something we see, hear, feel, smell, taste, or any combination of these senses. They can be something that occurred during an event that becomes permanently linked to that experience. When the trigger occurs, we can vividly recall the feelings and many times experience the physical components of the original experience. This happens when a song reminds us of a past romance, or when we hear the national anthem and see our country's flag.

Triggers or anchors can illicit extremely strong emotional and physical responses. Consequently, they are used extensively in sports. They can stimulate an athlete to remember a past triumph and return him to that winning state. We as speakers can use these same techniques to reduce tension, gather inner strength, and even enhance our delivery skills.

How

Triggers are usually created unintentionally. We unconsciously associate a trigger with an event. When the trigger randomly occurs, we experience the original sensations. This may cause some unusual reactions, like the hunger we feel just after deciding we're not hungry. Do you think those food commercials are working?

We can consciously create triggers, either at the time of the original experience or by using a mental creation of the desired event. At the peak of the experience, the trigger should be set. An example might be making a clenched fist at the moment of victory in a tennis game. We are capturing that winning feeling. Next time we step on the court, we make a fist, which triggers the same memory. Now we've returned to the physical and mental state we were in when we played well. Sound simple? It is.

What if you never had a successful experience to create the trigger? In that case just visualize the success and when you feel the peak of the imagined experience, anchor away. This works because your mind can't tell the difference between actual events and vividly imagined ones.

For speakers, touching the thumb and first two fingers is probably the best and easiest anchor to establish. Picture yourself in front of an audience successfully giving the best presentation of your life. Hear your voice, feel the satisfaction you would knowing you did a great job. Then touch your fingers together strongly. Anchor! Do this at least 5 times, smiling as you achieve success. Clear your mind and then recreate the experience using all the senses. That's all there is to it. Maybe you've seen athletes visualize a desired performance, then smile when they have it just right. They are anchoring. It's that easy.

Triggers should be unique in some way because if they're used too often or in inappropriate situations, they will lose effectiveness. Also, after every success they should be refreshed and reinforced by touching the trigger again to re-link the winning feeling and experience.

Summary

When we first learn of a speaking opportunity, we need to keep our self-talk positive. We never let our inner voice undermine our self-confidence. As you prepare, keep your self-talk on your side. We should practice out loud at least twice, visualize ourself giving the presentation. Picturing ourself facing the audience, smiling. Hearing our voice and imagining our confident feelings. We do the presentation perfectly in our mind. Never making a mistake. If we do, we can back up our mental pictures and correct the error. When we have done it just right, we touch our thumb and first two fingers together. Anchoring!

While waiting to speak, visualize walking to the podium, turning to face the audience, delivering the message and finally visualize the great feeling of a job well done. Tell yourself how good it will be and how much the audience will enjoy your talk. Keep your mind totally engaged with the mental image and positive self-talk. When you rise to speak, anchor. Use the trigger as you need it, during the talk. That's all there is to psyching-up. Remember, the good speaker usually just prepares the material, while the great speaker also prepares the mind.

Chapter 9

JUST BEFORE SPEAKING

"Do what you can, with what you have, where you are." -- Theodore Roosevelt

The big day has finally arrived. This is the time to begin concentrating on your task. It begins with traveling to the speaking site. On the way, you can go over the opening and closing portions of your speech. Running through the main points also prepares your mind for the presentation.

Arrive early and get familiar with the room and the equipment. An unfamiliar room can make you feel uncomfortable. Just a few minutes taken to get the feel of the room, can do wonders. Set up any equipment you may need before anyone arrives. This helps you look cool, calm and collected.

The Room and the Equipment

Cheryl was preparing for a speech contest. She went to every location where the contests were scheduled and made each room her friend. This made her feel more comfortable and relaxed which contributed to her victories. Although most people will not be entering speech contests, if this approach can relax someone under that kind of pressure, it certainly will help relieve some of the discomfort many people feel when in an unfamiliar place. There are additional advantages to going over the presentation in the place where it will be delivered. One is making sure we'll be seen and heard by checking the audio-visual equipment and room acoustics. The second is running through the entire presentation one more time with the actual equipment being used. This gives you both increased confidence and a professional smoothness that only comes by being familiar with material and equipment.

Always arrive early at the speaking site to test the equipment. And if you're unsure, bring your own equipment to be sure you'll have something that works and avoid last minute hassles. JoAnn remembered the importance of bringing her own equipment. "I had to go to Texas to give a major presentation. I couldn't go early so I took my own projector and slides, even though on the phone they said 'Sure, we have a slide projector.' When I arrived, they had some old-time, funny projector. Everyone else had to put their slides into a different tray. Not me, I just set up my own projector and gave the only presentation that went well. By the way, I'm the only one they asked back."

Rapport

Once you have your equipment set up, you can begin meeting people as they arrive. This contributes to your confidence by allowing you to gather information about the audience, which, in turn, allows you to customize your talk to the listeners. You can then give examples and use names of audience members. This helps build rapport with them.

Rapport is one of those intangible factors that is critical to relaxing and bonding with the audience. Good rapport establishes a positive speaker-audience relationship. Rapport allows the speaker to build support before beginning to speak. It also relaxes both the speaker and audience by developing a bond through which ideas and opinions can be exchanged. It's the openness you feel with people you like and accept.

Breathing

Correct breathing can help control any nervousness you may be feeling by controlling the pre-speaking energy build-up. This can be accomplished by the use of diaphragmatic breathing. Our diaphragm is located about three inches above our waist, just below our rib cage. Put your hand on your stomach and breathe slowly. Try it now. Notice how relaxed you feel as you control your breathing. Of course it's not necessary to have your hand on your stomach to practice after becoming aware of how to control your breathing pattern.

This same relaxation can be obtained just before you speak by relaxing and using this method for about two to three minutes. Focusing your eyes on an object will help control the tempo of breathing even under stressful conditions. Concentrate on rhythmic breathing. This is also the time to control the inner voice. Repeating the affirmations that support you centers your mind and body on the task ahead. You should start breathing control anytime you feel nervousness begin. Forget reading your notes, you most likely won't remember any more than you knew earlier. Now is the time to put everything aside and focus on mind/body control.

Controlling the pattern of breathing has a strange calming effect. Breathing is something that normally is done at an unconscious level. By controlling the breathing rate, you can gain control of some of your other unconscious body reactions, such as the premature production of adrenaline. As you remember, that causes excess energy build-up, which is often misconstrued as nervousness. Slow rhythmic breathing will keep you in control.

Summary

Focus on the task ahead by reviewing the material on the way to the presentation. Arrive early and check out the room and the equipment. Introduce yourself to people as they arrive, get to know them and engage them in conversation. While actually waiting to speak, control your breathing and keep the self-talk positive. Used in concert, these techniques will have a major effect on your speaking performance.

Chapter 10

DELIVERY SKILLS

"Actions speak louder than words." — *- - Your Parents*

This chapter will cover the physical skills and techniques necessary to deliver your message with the greatest effectiveness and impact.

The delivery of the message is putting ideas, preparation and commitment into action. We constructed our message by carefully determining the purpose and then considering the audience. We followed the organizational format and prepared appropriate visual aids. Our practice has been effective. We arrived early and checked the room and equipment. Now it's the time for action.

It actually begins a few minutes before we rise to speak. Our mental preparation now becomes the major tool for getting ourselves ready. Our self-talk should be something like: "This will be great. They're going to really like it." These words support our desire to deliver the message. Then we visualize our performance with all its subtleties. Now is the moment we must physically stand up and make the message come to life.

The moment we rise to approach the lectern or front of the room, our delivery actually begins. Our stride and posture begin to influence the audience. The difference between the hesitant approach with eyes downcast and the purposeful stride with upright posture and face turned slightly towards the audience tells them if we're ready or not. Then slowly turn to face the entire group. Take a deep breath and smile with inner confidence. Now, the next phase begins.

Breath

We first face the audience and take a slow easy breath while the audience gets set and focuses on us. This pausing and gathering of strength displays personal confidence. In these first few seconds the speaker is saying, "I'm ready and I have an important message. It's time to be quiet and listen."

Smile

A smile is one of the first gestures we use to make direct contact with our listeners. This tells the audience that we're friendly, confident and prepared. It also opens a window of receptivity, because we accept ideas and information most readily from those people who, we believe, like us and who seem friendly. Our ideas may be so important and overwhelming that everyone must listen; however, often we need all the help we can get. A smile is also one of the most effective tools to establish a high level of rapport.

Gestures

When we stand in front of an audience, we are transmitting messages with both our words and body language. Many times people transmit different messages through these two channels. This incongruency undermines the speaker's credibility. Gestures and body language are unconscious ways people evaluate us. If we say that we believe in something and our body shows a defensive posture, people will tend not to believe us. Hands locked together in front of the body is a typical defensive posture. The so-called "Fig leaf" is closed and protective. A much better stance is to have your feet slightly offset, one foot a few inches ahead of the other and about 6-inches apart. Hands held loosely at the side is the best beginning position and a good neutral return stance. This position looks very relaxed and allows freedom to make effective gestures. Hands add important emphasis to our presentation. Practice hand gestures before a talk, but during a speech just let the gestures flow. It's similar to the concept described in the book, "The Inner Game of Tennis," by W. Timothy Gallwey. Practice the correct way to accomplish something. Then just relax and do what comes naturally.

Effective gestures result from knowing the material thoroughly. Then we don't need to worry, we simply stop trying to control gestures and let them flow. If we try to force gestures mechanically, we may end up emphasizing the words a split second after they are spoken. This slight delay looks awkward, which hinders effectiveness and undermines credibility.

The way we stand sets the stage for the audience's evaluation of our attitude. If we're slumped over or facing even slightly away from the audience, they will get the impression that we're uneasy or unsure of ourselves. Good posture and a straight on stance will add to our reception and helps us breathe effectively. When asking the audience for questions or support, an open stance with arms apart is appropriate. We may want to use a finger to point, but don't shake it at the audience. We may want to make a fist to show strength, but don't threaten.

When we finish our presentation, we should pause for a moment, make strong eye contact with the audience, then walk away with a look of confidence. Effective speakers don't shake their head and act as if they've blown it. They maintain that cool confident look even after sitting down. If we too keep an air of confidence, soon we actually begin to feel more confident. However, it can work either way. Acting less confident, can be a downward spiral. Whether it's up, or down is up to us. We need to evaluate what we want to accomplish, then use the posture and natural gestures that invite the desired response.

Eye Contact

The eyes are the windows of the soul. This age old adage may understate the importance of the eyes in communication. Eye contact is perceived to be a direct indication of our honesty and credibility. It begins when we first walk toward the speaking position with our heads turned slightly toward the audience. This "cheating," as it is called, gives the audience its first contact with the speaker and begins the bonding process. When finally reaching the speaking position and fully facing the audience, we again establish strong eye contact.

Many of us were told in school to look over the heads of the audience. This isn't at all effective. People sense the lack of true contact. We need to look at people individually. This encourages the feedback necessary to know how we are coming across and lets them bond with us. The speakers head and eye movement should be smooth and directed, pausing momentarily at the left, right and center of the audience. We have the ability to use macro-vision, seeing the entire audience at once, or micro-vision, which allows us to focus on each individual. Micro-vision makes it more like one-on-one communication many times over, rather than one to a large group. Micro-vision is a more personal type of eye contact, which relaxes the speaker and helps deliver the message in a conversational style.

Eye contact also establishes a bond with the group. This bonding is a form of rapport which can sway audiences and establish a speaker's point against strong opposition. Rapport is enhanced by the smile and a simple nod of the head. Rapport can bring diverse opinions closer together. It starts with individual eye contact, for about 4 to 5 seconds, followed by feedback from the audience in the form of a smile, nod or other non-verbal reply. To increase the potential for bonding, smile and nod. Bonding comes from our eyes and connects directly with the audience's hearts and souls.

Voice

The sound and inflection of our voice contributes approximately 35% of our message. Vocal changes can influence the entire meaning of words and sentences. Total voice control is a study far beyond the scope of this book, but lets us focus just on the basic elements that contribute the majority of the vocal effect. Using the voice like a musical instrument is a skill that comes with listening to our own voice. A tape recorder can do wonders. By recording ourselves, we can begin hearing vocal inflections and pitch.

To find your own natural voice, try this exercise. Sit in a chair with your feet flat on the floor. Bend over and read aloud from a book you have placed on the floor. Use a recorder or have a friend listen to your voice. Now, stand up and read the same passage again while continuing to record or with your listener carefully evaluating the sound of your voice. Was there a difference? Our natural voice is the one bending over while sitting in the chair. This posture forces us to speak from our diaphram. When people stand and deliver a speech, many times they speak from their throats, thus creating a different sound and straining the voice. This is not our natural voice, and using our throat for any length of time can be quite irritating and cause temporary loss of voice. If you perceive a problem, we suggest you start by reading some of the excellent books in this field such as Toastmasters' *Your Speaking Voice* or *Change your Voice - Change your Life* by Dr. Morton Cooper. Change of course takes concerted effort and practice, but it can be done. Some people may want to enroll in a voice improvement class. There are also many fine private coaches available.

Pace

Delivery speed should vary depending on the message. Some ideas or thoughts don't require much audience contemplation, while other concepts are delivered more slowly and directly for impact. Varying the pace or speed also helps keep interest up. Marked speed changes, along with well-timed pauses, are great attention getters. Both entertain and help the audience understand the message.

Pauses

Pausing from time to time will gain audience attention, emphasize a point and exercise audience control. The benefits of purposeful pausing are many and varied. The pause is something we can adjust rather easily once we have recorded our voice. Many people use filler words such as, and, so and ah, instead of pauses. These extra words add nothing to the presentation. A pause used to think or to allow the audience to mentally summarize, is far more effective than filler words. Some people believe that if they just keep talking, they'll hold attention. This is simply not true. Varied pace and pausing are much more effective and powerful speaking tools.

Enthusiasm

"*Nothing great was ever achieved without enthusiasm*" Emerson said. Enthusiasm is the ingredient that makes us special; it takes us away from being dull and boring. It lights up our face, it's the catalyst that makes a presentation special. It's true we all need the spark of enthusiasm to help us perform better. If we don't have this spark when speaking, our performance will be dull and lifeless. Sometimes it's hard to get enthusiastic about a speaking assignment. Yet it is this fire within that allows us to add vitality to our talks. We aren't just talking about excitement. Enthusiasm goes deeper. It's a passion. It isn't always the "rah rah" type. It's the spirit and sparkle within that wins hearts.

In training situations, the element of enthusiasm is the most difficult to convey. It must come from an attitude that says, "I love what I'm doing. I believe in my company and what I'm saying today." What if we don't feel this way? Act as if we do. It's surprising how much enthusiasm we will begin to demonstrate. Think about how you could express enthusiasm during a presentation.

Commitment

"People are convinced more by the depth of our commitment than the height of our logic." - Cavett Robert. People make decisions based on many different factors. The ancient Greeks described the factors as Ethos, Pathos and Logos. Begin by establishing personal credibility. This should be accomplished during the introduction of the speaker or during the opening of the presentation. Next, appeal to the emotions by demonstrating personal commitment to the idea or proposal. Finally, present the logic by giving the facts and information that support the position. This formula contains the elements of success that have been proven for thousands of years.

In business, people like to believe that all decisions are based on facts and logic alone. However, many times a hunch or other feelings invades the decision making process and sways the outcome. This occurs at both the conscious and subconscious levels much more often than people realize. Acceptance of this truism will allow us to understand the importance of demonstrating our commitment to a proposal or project. If we really don't believe in something, we need to try to find some part that we can support, or try to change the focus of the presentation. If we don't do it now, our insincerity will show later, perhaps unconsciously. If we show our audience that we believe, then they'll be much more likely to believe.

Confidence

We need to show confidence when we rise to speak, as we approach the speaking location and as we turn to face the audience. It's demonstrated the moment we make contact with the audience. Strong eye contact, a slow deep breath and a smile are the traits of a confident speaker. Dress well, smile, stand tall and confidence will radiate. Our mind set is - "we have prepared and have important information to share with the audience. They need the information and we can deliver." We must believe in ourselves and have our inner-voice support us. Acting confident even if we don't feel that way. This is what makes us appear confident and then to actually become confident.

Summary

Delivery skills are a combination of physical techniques such as; gestures, eye contact and voice inflection combined with commitment and enthusiasm. Mastering the physical skills requires awareness and practice. Enthusiasm and commitment must come from within. They are inner generated and cannot be taught. Yet, by "acting as if" we were enthusiastic and committed, we can begin to believe and respond as if we really were. These two are most important because they are the ones that sweep an audience away. We must be committed and enthusiatic about our message to master the skills of speaking.

Chapter 11

VISUAL AIDS

"One picture is worth a thousand words." -- Chinese proverb

There are some speakers with the rare ability to make any subject clear with words alone. However, most of us need some help. Visual aids can transform ideas, feelings and knowledge into communication that is much more understandable and effective.

We know that everyone's mind works differently. Many people think in pictures rather than words. These people relate more to visual stimulation than to the written or spoken word. In order to effectively communicate with them, we need to appeal to their sense of sight with pictures. They can understand ideas quickly when they are presented visually. Yet many speakers still try to communicate only with words.

Dr. Albert Mehrabian, a communications researcher at U.C.L.A., stated, and then scientifically proved, that there are three elements to communication, each impacting what the audience receives and comprehends. The three parts are the verbal message, the vocal message and the visual message. Strangely, the verbal, or actual words, accounts for only 7% of the message, the vocal, or the way we say the words, accounts for 38% and the visual image accounts for 55% of the message. Our body language, our facial expressions and all other non-verbal elements are visual and have a major impact on our audience. While most people are unaware of this, it is true and it has been proven many times. A recent study at the University of Minnesota, revealed that a presentation with visual aids is 43% more memorable and persuasive.

There are two aspects of visual communication. The first is the ability we possess to bring a message to life through our delivery skills using: gestures, motions, and words to create mental pictures. The second dimension is the use of visual aids to reinforce our message and to entertain the listener. Visual aids support our delivery skills and make almost any presentation more effective. We are not suggesting that visual aids replace the speaker, as happens so often with packaged programs, but rather that they are used to reinforce the content of the message.

Visual aids provide many benefits to both the speaker and the listener when used correctly. Here are just a few of the benefits:

- Message is more understandable because it is sent twice, once verbally and once visually.
- Speaker can control the listener's attention.
- Helps the speaker stay on track.
- Retention of the message is increased.
- Listener is visually stimulated.
- Time is saved.
- Advance preparation is required getting the speaker to prepare earlier.

In creating visual aids there are some simple, yet important, guidelines to follow. We do not have to create a masterpiece. The purpose of the visual aid is to stimulate the listener's mind and imagination, not to prove our skill as an artist. Some of the most effective visual aids are extremely basic. However, if the presentation is very important, we should get the assistance of a professional. If our company has a graphic arts department, we can consult them for help.

The best visual aids are pictures and symbols, not words. This includes charts and graphs which should be simple, clean and colorful. Sometimes there may be a need to use words. There may be no picture or symbol that clearly describes the subject. Yet in most cases, a picture or symbol is more effective and stronger. Be creative.

A few years ago we were working with a management development group. They conducted a survey of 25 major companies and wanted to identify each company before presenting the results. The team listed the names on an overhead transparency using a typewriter to compose the visual. The list was very long and the names small. Consequently, the graphic display was too complex and very dull. We suggested making a collage, using the companies' logos to create an interesting and visually entertaining overhead. This added a little color and some dynamics. It also challenged the audience to recognize each logo.

We will discover that the simpler the visual aid, the easier it is to understand. The easier to understand, the more involved the listener becomes. At the end of this chapter there is a list of different types of visual aids and how they might be most effectively and appropriately used. Next are some basic considerations, when creating visual aids.

Designing Them:

1. Keep it simple (one idea per visual).
2. Bigger is better.
3. Use only key words and phrases.
4. Use symbols or pictures when possible.
5. Use color to highlight important material (it aids retention and motivates).
6. Rule of six (six lines maximum).
7. Use minimum number of curves and grid lines (simplify charts).
8. Eliminate supplementary notes (save them for the report or handout).
9. Never exceed 40 characters across.
10. Printing is best. Avoid vertical lettering.

If our presentation uses an audio-visual device, we need to understand how it operates. When using any kind of mechanical aid: a slide, movie, overhead projector, PA system or VCR and monitor, remember "Murphy's Law" which says "Anything that can go wrong will go wrong" applies. We add "Does Go Wrong." To minimize the chance of things going wrong, we must practice with the equipment several times in advance so we know how to make it work with our eyes closed or close to it. Also, it is very helpful in smoothing out transitions caused by starting or stopping equipment, to work with a friend or co-worker, who can assist with the lights and switches. ALWAYS have an extra bulb, extension cord and spares of other vital equipment available.

Mechanical aids can be very useful but also very detrimental if they fail or go wrong. Practice with them many times. Master them, so that they support, not hinder. Exhibits, samples or models fall into the above category. While extremely helpful in getting our message across, they can also destroy efforts to accomplish effective communication. If you aren't sure how to make them work correctly, they can be not only embarrassing but, a total distraction. If you don't take the time to learn how to work the equipment correctly don't use it.

Above all, be sure the visual aid demonstrates or supports what we are saying, while we are saying it. We need to remove it from view, when we move on to the next point. Don't hand out or pass around anything to the audience during a presentation. Distributing material during a presentation, or even before, will distract attention from the speaker. The audience may begin to talk among themselves, read, get ahead of you or just fiddle. They might drop out completely and the message will be lost.

Using Them:

1. Plan ahead (rehearse with visuals).
2. Transport visuals and equipment yourself.
3. Make sure everybody can see.
4. Dramatize by underlining, circling and writing on visuals.
5. Control disclosure of information (reveals, overlays, write-ins).
6. Maintain eye contact with the audience.

While a visual aid may serve as notes or an outline, don't fall into the visual aid trap. Don't stare at the, visual, or keep looking back at it as if it were going to change in some way. We know what our aid says and how it looks. We need to keep our eyes on the audience intead of the visual. That way we maintain contact with them and receive feedback on how the message is being received.

Types of Visual Aids

A visual aid is anything that helps illustrate our ideas. There is no right or wrong visual aid, just the most appropriate. The visual aid that is displayed or used correctly heightens the chances for success. Short presentations, less than 15 minutes, should stay with a single type of visual aid otherwise the audience can get lost in the show. Longer presentations provide the opportunity to mix visual-aid mediums. This also can help keep the audience interested and alert.

Flip Charts

Requires an easel or stand

- Works well with groups less than 25
- Can be prepared in advance
- Can be created spontaneously (if you elect to create, use a pencil to ghostwrite in advance, this insures correct spacing)

Chalk or Marker Board

- Like the flip chart, can be prepared in advance
- No chance for ghostwriting
- Watch letter and line angle

Overhead Projector

Requires projector, table and screen

- Very little to go wrong
- Excellent visual aid
- Works well with small to large groups (100 or more) with proper lens and screen size
- Transparencies can be prepared ahead and high-lighted during display

Slides

Requires projector, table, tray, screen, and remote control.

- Medium to large groups
- Very professional
- Credible
- Comprehensive
- Must darken room
- Limited flexibility and extensive lead time

Movies

Requires projector, table and screen

- Medium to large groups
- Complete message
- Very professional
- Little speaker preparation
- Must darken room
- Very expensive
- Totally inflexible

VCR and Monitor

Requires complex equipment

- Small to medium groups
- Easy to review
- Very professional
- Slows action well
- Expensive
- Requires technical expertise

Exhibits, Samples and Models

Requires little or no room for set-up

- Small to medium groups
- Demonstrates how things work
- Attractive and fascinating
- Distracting if passed around
- Embarrassing if doesn't work

Charts and Graphs

- Requires advance planning
- For all size groups
- Adds credibility
- Simplify complex ideas

Line chart

- Lots of data over time
- Shows fluctuations

Bar chart

- Best comparing data
- High-light important data

Pie chart

- Draws attention to significant data
- Simple
- Delineates by percentage

Summary

Too many speakers rely only on the spoken word to communicate their knowledge, interest and excitement. The results can be disastrous. The speaker with no visual aids can lose contact and involvement with the audience. Additionally, many people understand and remember information presented in pictures rather than words. Visual aids should be used whenever possible, whether it's a one-to-one or one-to-a-group situation. Speakers are not replaced by the visual aids, they are supported by them.

Chapter 12

THE STRATEGY

"Success doesn't depend upon who you are or what you have; it depends on what you know and how you use it." *-- Mike Young*

We have condensed much of the information from the previous chapters into this strategy. The book and strategy come from studying outstanding speakers and determining how they first prepare, what they do just before they speak, and the skills with which they deliver the speech.

By mentally organizing the speaking tasks and thoughts into this sequence, we can quickly pattern our preparation and delivery after the very best speakers. The idea of copying patterns has been described as modeling in a number of books under the general umbrella of Neuro-Linguistic Programming. We believe this is the most effective way to learn any skill and this book is based on those methods.

Preparing

1. *Identify Purpose*

a. What is our prime objective? (specifically defined)

b. What do we want to accomplish? Persuade? Inform? Inspire? Entertain?

c. Check to make sure you can support that purpose. If not, decline the speech.

2. *Analyze Audience*

a. Who are they? Age, educational level, occupation, etc.

b. What are their attitudes toward, and knowledge of, the subject?

c. What is format of the presentation? Time limit, dress, Q & A?

d. The more we know the better.

3. *Gather Material*

a. Research: books, newspapers, reports, interviews.

b. Find some evidence: a statistic, fact, expert, analogy.

c. Personal stories and examples that illustrate the points.

d. Evaluate material against the audience. Will they like it? Is it understandable?

4. *Organize Material*

a. Use an outline and keep it simple.

b. Select a few key points (three are best).

c. Closing summary or call for action?

d. Does all the material support purpose?

e. Compare with audience. What will help them understand it? What visual aids?

5. *Practice*

a. Stand up and speak out loud. Practice where speaking. (if possible).

b. Practice the whole speech, for time and content. At least three times. Use visual aids and tape recorder.

c. Don't start at 9:30 the night before.

d. It's not just the desire to be successful but the will to prepare and practice that enhances our performance.

6. *Visualization*

a. Picture the room, walking to the front and being totally successful. Hear the applause. Feel good about the performance. Repeat several times.

b. Intensify the image and experience. Anchor it! (index & middle fingers with thumb).

c. Remember past successes. If there are none, imagine one and then act the way you would after a great success. Anchor.

Just Before

7. *Mental Rehearsal*

a. Begin to focus on the task ahead.

b. Relax, run through opening and closing.

c. Mentally practice before it counts.

d. Go through main points. Smile.

8. *Get the feel of the room*

a. Get there early and make the room your friend. A strange place can be intimidating to even the best speakers.

b. Check the equipment. Nothing destroys confidence faster than things not working right (bring spare bulbs and cords).

c. Make sure everyone can see visuals.

d. Make sure that they can hear in last row.

9. Get to know someone

a. A friendly face can relax us.

b. Talking to someone takes our mind off speaking for a few minutes.

c. We may find information that we can use later.

d. Use their name and information in the presentation to establish good rapport.

10. Visualize

a. While waiting, picture yourself in front of this group.

b. See the performance and the audience reacting favorably.

c. Imagine the feeling of doing a great job.

d. Hear your words.

11. Inner voice

a. Control the inner voice. Make it supportive.

b. Say "I command you to be totally resourceful. This will be great. They are going to really like this."

12. Anchor

a. This is the trigger that makes us resourceful and confident by recalling past successes.

b. Touch middle, forefinger & thumb together.

c. Repeat three or four times.

d. This brings it all together.

During

13. Smile

a. The first thing we do (unless the subject is inappropriate).

b. If we feel tension, smile.

c. We are receptive to ideas from people we like and who seem friendly.

d. Of all the things we wear, our smile is the most important.

14. Take a deep breath

a. The pause allows us to get ready and get the audience's attention to focus on us.

b. It just might be the most important breath we take.

c. It relaxes both us and the audience.

15. Eye contact

a. Establishes a bond with the audience.

b. It increases rapport and establishes an energy flow.

c. Eye contact is important for trust and believability.

d. See the audience as individuals, not just as a sea of faces.

e. Eyes are the mirror of the soul.

16. Anchor

a. Use it just when getting up to speak.

b. It is the strongest lever or tool you have.

c. During presentation (if we need extra strength).

17. Concentrate on the message

a. People will sense your desire to communicate.

b. Don't worry about how you are doing.

c. Focus on the importance of the message.

d. Show you care that they understand.

18. Be Committed

a. People are convinced more by the depth of your commitment than by the height of your logic.

b. If you're not committed, act as if you are.

c. Be enthusiastic. Enthusiasm means fire within.

d. People judge you more at the unconscious level than at the conscious level.

Summary

This speaking strategy is the way most successful speakers prepare and deliver their messages. It may not be the only way, but it has been proven over and over again. There are undoubtedly good speakers who would say they don't do these things listed in the strategy, yet when carefully questioned, they reveal that they themselves don't know how they are accomplishing the task. The fact is that many things in life are done at an unconscious level. An example is driving. We did a study of top level racing drivers and got a wide range of responses on what it takes to be a champion, yet by careful and scientific questioning, we found an underlying common strategy for success. It's the same with most learned skills. There is a strategy for excellence. Your task, if you want to become skillfull at anything, is to find the correct strategy and then use it. This speaking strategy , correctly used, will open the door to **SUCCESS for YOU.**

Sharing ideas that matter with people that care. —*Mike and Tom*

Last Thoughts

Throughout this book we have quoted from many famous and successful people. We have also used examples from real life situations featuring others perhaps not as famous or successful. In all of these cases, the underlying theme is that people are apprehensive and awkward when first attempting to master the skill of public speaking. Unfortunately, because of these feelings, many people have withdrawn from attempting to further participate in formal speaking situations. Many of these people have been left standing in the forgotten shadows of life.

John was identified by all his supervisors as a good employee with excellent potential. However, when given opportunities to contribute his ideas, he would shy away. When trying to find the key to unlock John's potential, he was sent to a variety of workshops and seminars. Eventually he was selected to attend an effective presentations skills workshop. His attendance was reluctant, one would say almost forced. His first attempt in speaking before the group was very traumatic. Yet, once he understood the importance of effective communications, was taught the skills of effective delivery, and was able to mentally prepare himself, he blossomed.

It was several months later in another workshop that we met John's old supervisor, and he told us the story of what had happened to John in the intervening months. The results were immediate and very apparent. John began to contribute his ideas, enthusiasm and commitment in a meaningful way. He was soon assigned to a team building project and was instrumental in gaining its acceptance. His confidence grew and he became program leader. Most of his suggestions were accepted and successfully implemented. The results were reason enough for advancement, recognition and reward, even in a very large corporation.

There are many roads to travel. The one we choose can make all the difference. Think how many people had the potential to make significant contributions and how many were lost for all time because of fear, anxiety, and lack of knowledge. Who will ever know?

Skill can be defined as the ability to effectively and readily use one's knowledge and abilities in the accomplishment of a desired performance. There is little we can perform, with any level of proficiency without knowledge and physical practice. This book has supplied the knowledge. We must now put this knowledge into action. This is done by rehearsing and then performing many times, and in many situations. We have referred to speaking as a learned skill. It is, and as such, we need to find or create opportunities to practice. They will help us master the skill of effective communications. For this is truly - **THE MOST POWERFUL SKILL A HUMAN CAN POSSESS.**

The excellence of performance lies not in far-a-way places but within ourselves, begging to be released.

"Oh God, grant us the serenity to accept that which cannot be changed, courage to change those things that should, and the wisdom to know the difference."

-- Reinhold Niebuhr

APPENDIX

The following pages address a variety of speaking situations and subjects. They represent tips and suggestions learned through years of experience. They can help deal with situations that arise with little or no warning. Review them, consider them and be prepared for what may happen when least expected. If we prepare for the unexpected, attempt to control what we can, and accept what we can't, we will be primed to successfully deal with life's many trials and tribulations.

Clothing

What to wear as a speaker is a frequent question. Just dress the same as, or slightly more formally than, the audience. If in doubt, overdress. We can always strip for action. A few years ago, the author was invited to speak to a group of union employees. Arriving in a three-piece suit, he became aware that the working group had a different dress code. Hard hats and boots predominated. What to do? Look at others and see what they are wearing. Luckily, the union officers were in attendance. Their vests were unbuttoned and their sleeves were rolled up. By removing the coat, loosening the tie, and unbuttoning the vest, the presentation was saved. The lesson is, if overdressed we can remove some of the finery. If we do not bring the correct clothes, we may be in deep trouble.

Jewelry sometimes can distract the audience. Don't wear anything flashy. The reflection or the sound from a piece of jewelry can detract from the message. Maybe it's a good luck charm, but save the celebration until the presentation is complete.

For men, the color should be dark blue for power, or lighter if the presentation is a celebration or a casual affair. Three piece suits allow an open coat. A coat should not be left open without a vest, unless of course, someone is a model for Gentlemen's Quarterly.

Women can dress with a little more variety. Gray and blue offer a nice variance without losing credibility. A contrasting blouse can add flash without detracting. Keep it simple and tasteful. Speaking situations are not fashion shows, but opportunities to show leadership and expertise.

Too tall, too short, too wide or too narrow? Go to a first class tailor and ask for help. Yes, it will cost more. However, we will get a first-class speaking outfit, one we will feel comfortable and confident wearing. When we stand to speak we will know the value of our investment. If it fits well and we feel good, it's worth whatever it costs.

Dialects

There are as many regional dialects as there are regions in our country. When speaking, clear and complete enunciation is important. A speaker with a Texas drawl, a Spanish accent or anything else that calls attention, produces a hypnotic-type fascination for the listener. These generally result in a positive response and tend to keep the interest of the audience.

For a person with an ear for music, an off key or sour note is as irritating as a fingernail scraped on a blackboard. The lazy G has the same effect on many people - - "talkin", "walkin", "thinkin", etc., it is the ING ending with no G. There is a tendency for people to unconsciously believe the speaker with the lazy G is uneducated, and therefore, unbelievable. We can use a tape recorder to listen for the lazy G or other verbal distractions. This also can be accomplished with the help of a friend who will stop and correct us each time we make a verbal error. This is similar to the kids' game in which; after saying "You know," they say, "No, I don't know. You're telling the story." This may be hard for the listener to do, but it will quickly allow the speaker to begin to hear the error in language. Once that occurs, the speaker can quickly correct.

Glasses

Those of us who wear glasses have a challenge. We must establish even stronger eye contact because our eyes are partly hidden by light reflection. This requires extra work and effort to hold contact longer and more directly. Sometimes we can remove the glasses for emphasis, but we must be careful not to play with them.

General Appearance

By all means, look in a mirror and sharpen up before speaking. A tie that is not correct or clothing that is in disarray can detract from a professional appearance. We need to make sure our hair is combed, our finger nails are clean and generally we should sharpen up just before speaking.

Humor

Should we use humor in a talk? If we ask this question, the answer is probably "no." This is not to say we may not say something that is spontaneously funny. Generally people who use humor successfully do it naturally. Don't use a joke you've just heard if you're not an experienced joke teller. You will feel and look awkward. The best business humor is spontaneous and can't be planned. Yes, humor can break the ice and relieve tension. But if you are uncomfortable using humor, you will only increase tension. Humor is good, but use it only if it's your style and you use it naturally.

Introductions

When called on to introduce someone, a few simple steps will prepare the audience and set the stage for the speaker. As a master of ceremonies introducing the next speaker, we need to spark audience interest by first explaining why the subject is important to the group. Asking a question, repeating a quotation, or just pointing out the pertinence of the subject are some of the best ways of arousing curiosity. Next, explain why the speaker is qualified. This usually incorporates experience as well as education. Hobbies and memberships may have some relevancy to the speaker's qualifications. Use items relevant to the topic. The title of the speech and the speaker's name finish the introduction. By giving the speaker's name last, we cue the speaker and we prompt the audience to applaud. As a meeting leader or host, be sure to lead that applause for those who did not get the cue. Be sure to check the pronunciation of the speaker's name.

Bill was once introduced by the master of ceremonies as being a close friend. Unfortunately, the host hardly knew the speaker and had not checked the pronunciation of Bill's unusual last name. When the moment came for Bill's name, a very poor and humorous attempt at the name was made. This was extremely embarrassing for both the host, who lost credibility, and the speaker, who had to correct the situation.

In formal situations most experienced speakers prepare their own introductions. This insures the appropriate message and credentials and that the right tone is set for the presentation. Also the host does not take too long or steal some of the speaker's thunder. Names can be spelled out phonetically, if they are unusual. Be sure to read the introduction out loud, before sending it, so we can be sure it sounds appropriate. Sometimes a written introduction sounds quite stilted when it's read out loud. One-half of a typed page or one minute in length, is about right.

Lectern

These devices were not made for the speaker, only the lecturer. Some might say they need a place to put notes. Resist the temptation to use them. They keep the speaker from establishing rapport with the audience. Fifty five-percent of the message is visual; let's not cut ourselves short. Lecterns are for use in schools where extensive notes are required. Most business talks should not require notes, or so few that they can be used as visual aids. When business meeting rooms were laid out, something was needed to show the speaker where to stand. Thus the lectern was suggested and a few salesmen got rich but, the rest of us got stuck with an ineffective device. Sometimes the controls for the slide projector are even built into the lectern. If this is the case, get another type of remote.

Last, but not least, is our posture. If we must use a lectern, we must stand up straight, the way our mother told us. Too many people lean on, or try to hide behind, the wooden edifice. That loses much of the potential audience contact. Stand up and touch the audience with your personality. Let us see and hear you.

Notes and Scripts

We don't recommend using a script unless making a press statement or other precise communication such as about a hazardous spill. In these instances a wrong word can have a major impact and communication with the public must be impeccable, with just the right message conveyed.

Notes can be used; however, their use should be limited to situations where a number of facts and statistics must be included. If possible, we recommend having those key facts put on visual aids. Notes reduce eye contact and consequently our rapport. For most presentations, it is more important to have strong rapport than to try and convey every single point of the talk. We find that speakers are far more effective without notes.

If they must be used, have them written in conversational style. Have them typed in large letters on 8½ by 11 inch paper. Don't staple the pages together but do number them. Include margin notes as a reminder to look up or cue other important actions.

Pointers and Markers

Don't hold anything in your hands that you could start playing with, such as a pointer, marking pen or even a pencil. If you have to use something during your presentation, plan where to pick it up and where to put it down. This advice goes for all types of hand- outs or models that you might want to demonstrate. One comment on light pointers. They may show any tremor in your hand. If you can avoid them, do so. If not, move them in a circle so any tremor is lost in the movement.

Questions and Answers

No matter how well we have prepared and delivered the presentation, we need feedback to determine what our listeners thought we said. A question-and-answer session provides that connection. It also affords the listeners an opportunity to adjust the information to their needs. Finally, it provides a chance to restate our message where it was unclear or to expand upon an area of particular interest to someone in the audience. To achieve these important objectives, certain techniques will insure our effectiveness and encourage audience participation. In business and community activities, there is often hostility and competition. We need to defuse the hostility and remain cool and calm under pressure.

Preparing for the questions requires reviewing the material to be presented, anticipating what might be asked and practicing the answers. Then the appropriate answer can be prepared or the main presentation may be modified to clarify the points raised. Having a preview presentation with friends or coworkers provides an opportunity to answer the obvious questions and indicates what information inspires questions.

Soliciting questions from an audience is an important part of an effective session. Open body language and a smile creates the atmosphere necessary to generate inquiries. This open body position is represented by a relaxed posture and opened arms in a welcoming gesture. Many of us can remember a situation where a speaker asked for questions with crossed arms and a frown. This type of body language contradicts the words. We need to be careful that both our words and body convey the same message. We must be congruent.

Encouraging a questioner by carefully listening to, and paraphrasing the question, shows we want to understand the question and are mentally engaged. We don't want to be too quick to answer, even if we understand the question. Be sure the questioner is finished, then pause and carefully frame the answer. People who answer too quickly are perceived as shooting from the hip and not thinking before they speak.

One of the most stressful situations arises when the speaker asks for questions and none are forthcoming. This is easily overcome by one of two strategies, or a combination of both.

The first and the easiest is to ask yourself a question. "A question frequently asked is..." or "You might ask..." This should break the ice.

The second method is to have a friend ask the first question. This can get the session off to a positive start. Don't be too obvious. Rewarding the questioner, regardless of who it is, helps encourage more questions. This can be done with a smile, a nod or a positive thank you.

Dealing with the questions themselves presents a challenge to clarify, embellish or restate. This ensures credibility. Probably the most difficult situation is when there are hostile members of an audience. The following rules and suggestions can guide us through the mine field of deceptive, leading and direct attack questions.

Keeping answers short and to the point allows more interaction with the audience and keeps the session moving. Begin with direct eye contact with the questioner, then move to the entire audience. The eye contact establishes strength and helps form a bond with the audience. It also serves as a tool to cut off contact with an obviously hostile person. Without eye contact most people will find it difficult to interject a question. If there is a hostile question, answer it directly, then look to another part of the room to cut off any more questions from that person. Admit that you don't know the answer to a question if you don't. Trying to wing it or faking an answer can discredit us, our company or our cause. No one has to know everything, and a smart person is not afraid to say he doesn't know. He may add, "Give me your card, and I'll get you the answer."

Avoid arguing. If two people enter a spitting contest, both get wet. Don't get into a debate. That does not mean that we have to let an untrue statement go un-challenged. If attacked, just state the facts and move on. If someone insults us, be the injured party. We'll gain audience sympathy. The question-and-answer session is one of the most important and rewarding. Practice before, anticipate, question and be open and friendly.

Room Environment

If we arrive early and check out the room, some problems can be eliminated in advance. Some rooms have limitations that may require adjustment. A long and narrow room may limit our movement or placement of visual aids. With a short and wide room, we may want to move into the audience instead of having to turn our back to part of the group. If we find the seating arrangement unacceptable, we can ask the audience to move. This should be done in a polite and non-threatening way, "I believe you could hear me or see me if you turned your chairs around," or, "We have a large room this morning; if everyone moves closer, I won't have to shout."

Adjusting the room environment to a comfortable temperature can make a significant difference on our audience's attentiveness. It is far better to have the room a little on the cool side, than too warm. If the sound of snoring requires us to speak louder, the room might be too warm. Lighting should also be adjusted. Darkened rooms can have the same effect on an audience as a warm one does. Listen for the same warning.

Sitting Down

At meetings it might not be appropriate to stand. In those situations we need to project a strong image and get our message across. To do this effectively, we need to maintain good posture and make strong eye contact. Pause to project the image of considering the situation before replying. Lean forward slightly before speaking. Posture, pausing, and eye contact are the keys to projecting the right image while sitting.

Speaking Impromptu

Sometimes we may be asked to speak, with little or no notice, about a subject that we have some expertise in. This can happen in meetings or in social and community involvement situations. The following steps will allow us to quickly organize our thoughts and then deliver an effective presentation:

1) Take a moment to pause and decide on a point of view. Whatever your position, make a choice and adhere to it.

2) Slowly rise to your feet. This moment will allow your mind time to organize ideas. It also gives you the appearance of considering the issue before speaking.

3) Pause and take a slow deep breath. The audience can then have a moment to focus and you can get set.

4) Start with a strong and clear statement.

5) Be committed.

6) Make solid eye contact. Bond with each member of the audience.

7) Illustrate your point with personal stories or experiences. Examples that use stories are both interesting and captivating. They can have profound impact, far beyond the first impression.

8) Set your course and stick to it instead of paddling frantically in all directions. (This piece of advice is good for many situations.) In an impromptu or short talk, it will keep you focused and to the point.

9) Conclude with a summary. This ties it all together. It will clearly tell the audience what you believe, feel, see or understand about the subject.

Time Limits

When we are given a time limit, it's important that we stick to it. Here is where practice pays off. If we have gone over our speech a few times, we will know the time required. Using a tape recorder can get the time down and let us listen to the talk later. All speeches should be a little short of the allotted time. Any speech that lasts after the meeting is scheduled to adjourn will fall on deaf ears. Also if the preceding speakers run overtime, we still will have time to get our point across. Designing our speech with three main points helps here, so that we can cut one or two and still have an opening, body and closing. Yes, the body will be short, but we will at least have some logic to our talk.

Keeping within the time limits will make us a more effective communicator and will make a friend of the program chairman. Mike was scheduled to give a one-hour presentation on how to build a dynamic organization. The preceding speaker ran 30 minutes overtime. No stretch break for the audience and 30 minutes of his time used. After being introduced, he asked everyone to stand up and stretch, knowing that the mind only can absorb what the seat can endure. With a cut here and a point passed over there, the speech finished only 2 minutes over the original scheduled time. The program chairman was thankful; and after the presentation, many people in the audience commented on Mike's thoughtfulness. They insisted that he return in the future and present whatever message he thought the group would enjoy. The lesson is, "a group will support us if we are considerate of them."

Words and Language

There is no such thing as a true synonym in the English language. No two words mean exactly the same thing. Words have their own nuances and tones, even when expressing the same concept. And many words have more than one meaning. One word may be more appropriate than another, depending on the particular context in which the word is used. "Fast" for example, can mean everything from quick to not eating. "Post" can mean everything from pole to mail. "Clear" can mean everything from bare to definite and understood and sunny to translucent. And, that is before one considers its use as a verb when it empties, exonerates, clarifies, surmounts, and repays.

The impact of the English language, on the landscape of the human mind, is broad and varied. We need to be precise. Even simple words mean different things to different people. Those differences, and presenters who do not compensate for those differences, lose effectiveness and credibility.

opening

purpose ______________

____

____

title ______________

____

key words

____

____

____

details

key words

____

____

____

details

key words

____

____

____

details

closing

How to obtain a copy of this book for your friends and for your organization.

Copies of this book are available directly from the publisher if not in your local bookstore.

1 copy @ $9.50

2-9 copies @ $7.95 each.

10-25 copies @ $6.95 each.

26 and over @ $6.00 each.

Postage and handling included.

Speaking for Effect

P.O. Box 966

Montrose, CA. 91021

Also available, is free information on workshops and seminars featuring the techniques described in this book. Call Speaking for Effect at 818-248-4807